THE PSALTER 1998

A Draft Text for *Common Worship*

GS Misc 544

THE PSALTER 1998

A Draft Text for *Common Worship*

 CHURCH HOUSE
PUBLISHING

Church House Publishing,
Church House,
Great Smith Street,
London SW1P 3NZ

ISBN: 0-7151-3823-5

Published 1999 by Church House Publishing

Printed by The Cromwell Press Ltd, Trowbridge, Wilts

Contents

Introduction

'The Church with psalms must shout, no door can keep them out'
wrote the poet and Anglican priest George Herbert in the early
seventeenth century, and in doing so he gave magnificent expression
to the desire to praise and lament which lies at the heart of all
Christian worship. Whether said or sung, the psalms have featured
at the core of the Church's worship from its earliest days. The inter-
pretation and understanding of some of the psalms have varied
radically over the centuries, as have approaches to the translation of
the psalms and their liturgical use. Yet the vividness of the imagery
evoked by the psalms and their range of expression and content
continue to ensure their place at the heart of the Church's worship.

The Psalter 1998 has been prepared by members of the Liturgical
Commission in consultation with some professional Hebraists and
musicians, and at the request of the General Synod. In a debate on
the liturgical publishing programme of the Church of England, held
during the Group of Sessions in November 1997, the General Synod
passed a resolution asking the Liturgical Commission to prepare a
draft of the entire psalter along the lines proposed in GS Misc 504, *A
New Psalter for Liturgical Use in the Church of England. The Psalter 1998:
A Draft Text for Common Worship* has been prepared as the first stage
of the Liturgical Commission's response to that request. It is a draft
text, open to public consultation and subject to further amendment
during the first half of 1999. The Liturgical Commission hopes to
publish a final text of the psalter proposed for *Common Worship* prior
to the November 1999 Group of Sessions of the General Synod.
The publication of *The Psalter 1998* is intended to encourage the use
of these draft psalm texts in public worship, and to provide an
opportunity for wide consultation. As the psalms form an integral
part of the Bible, they do not require authorization from the General
Synod for their use in public worship in the Church of England.
However, because the Liturgical Commission is seeking to provide a
psalter which is particularly suitable for use alongside the new
Common Worship liturgical provision, it is seeking comment at this
stage from as wide a public as possible as to the appropriateness of
this version of the psalms for use in public worship in the Church
of England today. The members of the Liturgical Commission would
encourage all those wishing to experiment with the use of texts in
The Psalter 1998 to do so and to let us know their views.

Should you wish to comment on the texts of the psalms in *The Psalter 1998* you should copy or photocopy the questionnaire on pages 251 – 253 of this book. Completed questionnaires should be sent before 15 June 1999 to the following address: The Secretary of the Liturgical Commission, Re **Psalter Survey**, General Synod Office, Church House, Great Smith Street, London, SW1P 3NZ. These comments will be taken into account as work continues on the draft psalter during 1999, ready for a further General Synod debate on the psalter which is provisionally scheduled for November 1999.

The psalms themselves are generally encountered by readers or hearers in two contexts. The Book of the Psalms lies at the heart of the Old Testament, and as such is translated, commented on and reflected on by Jew and Christian alike. Within the traditions of Christian worship, however, the psalms have been gathered together in their own liturgical book, *The Psalter*. These differing contexts for reading and using the psalms have led to differing ways of approaching questions of translation from the original Hebrew of the psalms. Biblical scholarship demands the critical application of the skills of Hebraists in assessing the merits of differing texts and styles of translation to arrive at an English text which is faithful to the original Hebrew and capable of being read silently or out aloud by a single voice. A psalter for liturgical use not only demands faithfulness to the Hebrew in the preparation of an English text, but also an acknowledgement of the corporate prayed traditions of using the psalms which have shaped the beliefs and experiences of worshippers for generations. Psalms used liturgically may be said or sung, by a single voice or by many voices, repeatedly day by day, week by week, and year by year. Thus, in the Church of England, the psalter published in *The Book of Common Prayer 1662* has been crucial not only in shaping Anglican liturgical memory but in profoundly influencing the development of the English language.

The psalter published in *The Book of Common Prayer 1662* is no longer universally used in the parishes of the Church of England. There have been services in contemporary language in the Church of England for many years, and the need for a contemporary language psalter to complement authorized Church of England liturgical provision was well met during the 1970s and 1980s with the publication of *The Psalms – A New Translation for Worship* (Collins, 1976). It is this psalter which is printed in *The Alternative Service Book 1980*. However, the new provisions of the *Common Worship* service books are marked by a style of language notably different to that of *The Alternative Service Book*. What is needed now is a contemporary language psalter which will complement the new provisions of the

Common Worship service books, and whose quality of language and imagery is capable of carrying the prayer of all those who delight to say or sing the psalms in their worship.

In November 1997 members of the General Synod debated the Liturgical Commission's report, *A New Psalter for Liturgical Use in the Church of England* (GS Misc 504). The report contained the draft text of fifty psalms, and was prefaced by an introductory essay which outlined the reasons underlying the preparation of a new contemporary-language liturgical version of the psalms in English. The introductory essay in GS Misc 504 was read by some as appearing to impugn the professional scholarship of those who had been involved in the preparation and publication of *The Psalms – A New Translation for Worship*, as it was originally called, and its later version, *The Liturgical Psalter: An Inclusive Language Version* (HarperCollins, 1995). Members of the Liturgical Commission deeply regret this. The scholarship of those who prepared *The Liturgical Psalter* is of the first order; as those who have worked on *The Psalter 1998* are glad to acknowledge.

In its preparations for its work on *The Psalter 1998* the Commission identified four principal criteria which it believes should characterize a psalter for liturgical use in the Church of England:

- The accuracy of the translation of the psalter from the Hebrew text in a way which is sympathetic to liturgical use within the traditions of the Church of England;

- The quality of the language on the tongue of those who sing and those who say the psalms;

- The memorability of the translation and its resonance with known psalter traditions in the Church of England;

- The accessibility of the language of the psalms to a wide range of worshippers.

With these criteria in mind, in 1995–6 members of the Liturgical Commission undertook to evaluate during the saying of the Daily Offices some of the most commonly used psalters in the Church of England. Amongst the contemporary language psalters which were used in the evaluation were *The Liturgical Psalter* (published in the ASB); *The Liturgical Psalter: An Inclusive Language Version*, published by HarperCollins in 1995; and the psalter published in *Celebrating Common Prayer* (a very mildly revised version of the psalter originally published in the Episcopal Church of the United States of America's *Standard Book of Common Prayer* in 1979). As a result of the period of evaluation, the Liturgical Commission came to recognize that no existing version of the psalter seemed to be entirely satisfactory, and that a new version of the psalter for liturgical use in the Church of England would be needed. In particular, the issue of how to handle inclusive language in the psalms needed to be addressed afresh. For further discussion on the development of the Church of England's policy on questions of inclusive language, see *Making Women Visible*, GS 859 (Church House Publishing, 1989), and *Language and the Worship of the Church*, GS 1115 (1994). The recommendations in the reports were endorsed by the General Synod in debates held in July 1989 and July 1994. In the light of these findings the Commission decided to undertake a substantial revision of the text of the ECUSA psalter, taking account of the slightly revised version published in *Celebrating Common Prayer*.

The criteria with which the Liturgical Commission have been working to revise the ECUSA text of the psalms have raised a number of complex issues, among them that of the process of translation. The original text of the psalms cannot always be recovered with certainty, and even when it can different translations may be possible. Ancient manuscripts generally lacked punctuation and – in the case of Hebrew – even vowels until about the eighth century AD. There was a firm oral tradition, but supplying these missing elements is some-times a matter of editorial decision rather than a given. Added to this, the Hebrew scriptures themselves were not regarded as static by their editors; rather, they were a living treasure, to be 'contemporized' and applied to new circumstances. The translation of the scriptures into Greek, the Septuagint (third century BC onwards), has a number of readings different from the main Hebrew tradition; for example, it sometimes reflects a more universalistic reading, appropriate for Jews involved in the life of Gentile cities. In Aramaic-speaking areas, where Hebrew was no longer generally spoken, there were Targums, creatively expanded paraphrases in Aramaic, which were read in synagogue after the Hebrew.

The New Testament writings were in Greek and usually followed the Septuagint, or other current Greek versions, sometimes with significant differences from the Hebrew, for example James' citation of Amos 9.11,12 at Acts 15.16,17; and at Ephesians 4.8 Paul quotes Psalm 68.18 in line with the Targum and not the Hebrew (see the Notes at the end of this book for more details). This flexibility in the use of the psalms may encourage us to revisit the task of 'contemporizing' scripture and not view it as a static museum piece; to seek for language which takes account of a developing tradition of use in a Christian context, including our contemporary context, rather than a purely literal accuracy. Where there is no certainty as to the original text and meaning, and where current Hebrew scholarship does not forbid, the Commission has chosen the translation which best fits both the criteria listed above and the tradition of developing theological understanding (see the Notes for examples).

The most challenging demand for contemporization arises from the patriarchal context of scripture and the dominance of male terms used generically (for example, 'man' or 'men' used to denote human beings in general). There is as yet no consensus in the Church on the subject of inclusive language, but the General Synod has agreed that liturgical texts should, where possible, avoid the use of terms which can be heard as exclusively male in respect of human beings. The guidelines agreed by the General Synod (*Language and the Worship of the Church*, GS 1115, 1994) do not, however, settle all questions. Some moves are easy, for example 'kindred' for 'brethren' (Psalm 122.8). Psalm 15 in *The Psalter 1998* shows how 'he, him, his' can be avoided without serious loss. But some substitutions for 'man' and 'men' may themselves have drawbacks, for example the use of the word 'mortals' is unsatisfactory when the contrast is between humans and God (for example Psalm 118.6). The question of how to handle 'man/son of man' (Hebrew *adam/ben adam*) raises the issue sharply, especially in Psalm 8 (see the Notes). In this instance the competing priorities of idiomatic translation, christological resonance and inclusive language are at odds with one another, and yet require a working resolution suitable for liturgical use. One way of inclusivizing the language of the psalms which the Commission has generally tried to avoid is the use of plurals; their over-use can blunt the particularity and immediacy of the text which are important. In general the Commission has adopted a mixed economy with regard to inclusive language, avoiding male terms where the meaning is clearly generic except where other factors, theological or linguistic, seem to weigh more heavily.

A related group of issues with which the drafting group has also had to grapple is the relationship of a contemporary-language psalter to its predecessors, especially within the Anglican prayed traditions of Coverdale's psalter as published in *The Book of Common Prayer 1662*. The Commission has aimed, broadly, to retain where possible the flavour of the language and rhythms of Coverdale's psalter, which are so bound up with Anglican ways of saying and singing the psalms. As a result the question of archaism and general accessibility has had to be faced squarely. Where words have changed their meaning and become unintelligible in their context in our own day they have been altered. But there is much which, while not current idiom, may still enhance the poetry and recitation of the psalms, for example Psalm 69.23 'They gave me gall to eat' (*The Psalter 1998*); and Psalm 114.5 'What ails you, O sea, that you flee away?'; and the reversing of pronoun and verb, 'They have a mouth, but cannot speak; eyes have they, but cannot see' (Psalm 115.5). There is a balance to be drawn between the use of sympathetic echoes of Coverdale's language and rhythms, and the development of a public rhetoric suitable for public worship today. Often, the Commission has kept familiar poetic phrases but only where the Hebrew warrants the translation; for example Psalm 137.6 'Let my tongue cleave to the roof of my mouth'. The translation of a number of such richly idiomatic words as *hesed* which defy the consistent use of any one English equivalent is given attention in the Notes.

Music

A selection of musical settings of a small number of psalms is printed in the Music Appendix. The settings include Anglican chant (with pointing), modal tones and Gregorian chant. Some musical settings include the use of repeated refrains. The settings are provided as examples of different ways of handling the psalm texts set to music. They are not intended to be a definitive range of settings. The psalms themselves have been selected from among those most commonly used (for example, at Morning Prayer and at Compline), and they represent a variety of psalm styles. The psalms in the Music Appendix are printed with antiphons which may be said or sung at the beginning and end of a psalm, and repeated after one or more verses as the psalm is recited. The Commission hopes eventually to provide such antiphons for all the psalms in *The Psalter 1998*. However, this is not to imply that antiphons need be used. The musical settings in the Music Appendix may be reproduced free of charge for use in worship, provided that full copyright acknowledgement is given on each occasion.

Public Comment

In addition to comment on technical issues of translation and the suitability of the texts for musical settings, there is a number of specific issues on which the Liturgical Commission would be glad to receive comment from those who use *The Psalter 1998*. These include:

(a) In *The Psalter 1998* the Liturgical Commission has decided not to bracket difficult verses in the psalms (in contrast with *The Liturgical Psalter* as published in *The Alternative Service Book*). The decision not to bracket difficult verses in the psalms is based on the grounds that the whole of the psalter is given to be prayed with and by the Church.

(b) The psalms are set out for recitation, with an asterisk * marking the half-way point in each verse. The Liturgical Commission believes that an asterisk may, in contrast to the colon, be a more noticeable means of marking the half-way point in each verse without detracting from the layout of the printed psalm on the page.

A questionnaire to all users of this book, with questions on these two points and others, is contained on pages 251 – 253.

The Gloria Patri

When using the texts of the psalms from *The Psalter 1998* in worship, the version of the Gloria Patri which may be used at the end of each psalm or group of psalms is:

> Glory to the Father and to the Son *
> and to the Holy Spirit;
> as it was in the beginning is now *
> and shall be for ever. Amen.

Acknowledgements

Members of the Liturgical Commission are indebted to a number of people who have given helpful advice during the course of the preparation of *The Psalter 1998* and its Music Appendix. Detailed comment on the entire Hebrew text of the psalms has been most generously provided by Mr John Eaton (formerly Reader in Biblical Studies, University of Birmingham). Musical settings of a select number of psalm texts have been written by a variety of composers named in the Music Appendix. For the contributions of these people and of other scholars, members of the General Synod and other correspondents to the Liturgical Commission we are very grateful.

+David Sarum
Chairman, The Liturgical Commission
December 1998

The Psalter

PSALM 1

1   Happy are they who have not walked
       in the counsel of the wicked, *
    nor lingered in the way of sinners,
       nor sat in the assembly of the scornful!

2   Their delight is in the law of the Lord, *
    and they meditate on his law day and night.

3   Like a tree planted by streams of water bearing fruit in due season,
       with leaves that do not wither; *
    whatever they do, it shall prosper.

4   As for the wicked, it is not so with them; *
    they are like chaff which the wind blows away
       from the face of the earth;

5   Therefore the wicked shall not be able to stand in the
       judgement, *
    nor the sinner in the congregation of the righteous.

6   For the Lord upholds the way of the righteous, *
    but the way of the wicked shall perish.

PSALM 2

1   Why are the nations in tumult? *
    and why do the peoples devise a vain plan?

2   The kings of the earth rise up,
       and the rulers take counsel together, *
    against the Lord and against his Anointed.

3   'Let us break their bonds asunder *
    and cast away their cords from us.'

4   He who dwells in heaven shall laugh them to scorn; *
    the Lord shall have them in derision.

5   Then shall he speak to them in his wrath *
      and terrify them in his fury.

6   'Yet have I set my king *
      upon my holy hill of Zion.'

7   I will proclaim the decree of the Lord; *
      he said to me: 'You are my Son; this day have I begotten you.

8   'Ask of me and I will give you the nations for your inheritance *
      and the ends of the earth for your possession.

9   'You shall break them with a rod of iron *
      and dash them in pieces like a potter's vessel.'

10   Now therefore be wise, O kings; *
      be prudent, you judges of the earth.

11   Serve the Lord with fear, and with trembling kiss his feet; *
      Lest he be angry and you perish from the way,
         for his wrath is quickly kindled.

12   Happy are all they *
      who take refuge in him!

PSALM 3

1   Lord, how many are my adversaries! *
      Many there are that rise up against me!

2   Many there are who say of my soul, *
      'There is no help for him in his God.'

3   But you, O Lord, are a shield about me; *
      you are my glory, and the one who lifts up my head.

4   When I call with my voice to the Lord *
      he will answer me from his holy hill;

5 When I lie down and sleep, *
  I rise up again, for the Lord sustains me.

6 I will not be afraid of tens of thousands of the peoples *
  that are set against me all around.

7 Rise up, O Lord and deliver me, O my God! *
  O that you would strike all my enemies upon the cheek,
   and break the teeth of the wicked!

8 Salvation belongs to the Lord: *
  May your blessing be upon your people!

PSALM 4

1 Hear me when I call, O God of my righteousness; *
  you set me at liberty when I was hard-pressed;
   have mercy on me and hear my prayer.

2 'How long will you people dishonour my glory; *
  how long will you love vain things and seek after falsehood?'

3 But know that the Lord has chosen to himself
   the one that is faithful; *
  when I call upon the Lord, he will hear me.

4 Stand in awe, and sin not; *
  commune with your own heart upon your bed, and be still.

5 Offer the sacrifices of righteousness *
  and put your trust in the Lord.

6 There are many that say, 'Who will show us any good?' *
  Lord, lift up the light of your countenance upon us.

7 You will put gladness in my heart, *
  more than when their corn and wine and oil increase.

8 I will lie down and sleep in peace; *
  for it is you, Lord, only, who make me dwell in safety.

PSALM 5

1 Give ear to my words, O Lord; *
consider my lamentation.

2 Hearken to the voice of my crying, my King and my God, *
for to you I make my prayer.

3 In the morning, Lord, you will hear my voice; *
early in the morning I make my appeal to you, and look up.

4 For you are the God who takes no pleasure in wickedness *
no evil can dwell with you.

5 The boastful cannot stand in your sight; *
you hate all those that work wickedness.

6 You destroy those who speak lies; *
the bloodthirsty and deceitful, O Lord, you abhor.

7 But as for me, through the greatness of your mercy,
    I will come into your house; *
I will bow down towards your holy temple in awe of you.

8 Lead me, O Lord, in your righteousness,
    because of my enemies; *
make your way straight before my face.

9 For there is no truth in their mouth;
    in their heart is destruction; *
their throat is an open sepulchre;
    they flatter with their tongue.

10 Declare them guilty, O God; *
let them fall through their own machinations.

11 Because of their many transgressions cast them out, *
for they have rebelled against you.

12 But let all who take refuge in you be glad; *
let them sing out their joy for ever.

13 You will shelter them, *
    so that those who love your name may exult in you.

15 For you, O Lord, will bless the righteous; *
    and with your favour you will defend them as with a shield.

PSALM 6

1   O Lord, in your wrath rebuke me not; *
    neither chasten me in your fierce anger.

2   Have mercy on me, Lord, for I am weak; *
    Lord, heal me, for my bones are racked.

3   My soul also shakes with terror; *
    how long, O Lord – how long?

4   Return, O Lord, and deliver my soul; *
    O save me for your loving mercy's sake.

5   For in death no one remembers you; *
    and who can give you thanks in the grave?

6   I am weary of my groaning; *
    every night I drench my bed
        and flood my couch with my tears.

7   My eyes are wasted with grief *
    and worn away because of all my enemies.

8   Depart from me all you that do evil, *
    for the Lord has heard the voice of my weeping.

9   The Lord has heard my supplication; *
    the Lord will receive my prayer.

10 All my enemies shall be put to shame and confusion; *
    they shall suddenly turn back in their shame.

PSALM 7

1   O Lord my God, in you I take refuge; *
    save me from all who pursue me, and deliver me;

2   Lest they rend me like a lion and tear me in pieces *
    while there is no-one to help me.

3   O Lord my God, if I have done these things: *
    if there is any wickedness in my hands,

4   If I have repaid my friend with evil, *
    or plundered my enemy without any cause;

5   Then let my enemy pursue me and overtake me, *
    trample my life to the ground,
       and lay my honour in the dust.

6   Rise up, O Lord, in your wrath;
       lift up yourself against the fury of my enemies. *
    Awaken, my God, the judgement that you have commanded.

7   Let the assembly of the peoples gather round you; *
    be seated high above them, O Lord, judge the nations.

8   Give judgement for me
       according to my righteousness, O Lord, *
    and according to the innocence that is in me.

9   Let the malice of the wicked come to an end,
       but establish the righteous; *
    for you test the mind and heart, O righteous God.

10   God is my shield that is over me; *
    he saves the true in heart.

11   God is a righteous judge; *
    he sits in judgement every day.

12   If they will not repent, God will whet his sword; *
    he will bend his bow and make it ready.

13   He has prepared the weapons of death; *
     he makes his arrows shafts of fire.

14   Behold those who are in labour with wickedness *
     who conceive evil and give birth to lies.

15   They dig a pit and make it deep *
     and fall into the hole that they have made for others.

16   Their mischief rebounds on their own head; *
     their violence falls on their own scalp.

17   I will give thanks to the Lord for his righteousness; *
     and I will make music to the name of the Lord Most High.

PSALM 8

1   *O Lord our governor, *
    *how glorious is your name in all the world! *

2   Your majesty above the heavens is praised *
        out of the mouths of babes and sucklings.

3   You have founded a stronghold against your foes; *
    that you might still the enemy and the avenger.

4   When I consider your heavens, the work of your fingers, *
    the moon and the stars that you have ordained,

5   What is man, that you should be mindful of him? *
    the son of man, that you should care for him?

6   You have made him little lower than the angels, *
    and crown him with glory and honour.

7   You have given him dominion over the works of your hands; *
    and put all things under his feet,

8   All sheep and oxen, *
    even the wild beasts of the field,

9   The birds of the air, the fish of the sea, *
     and whatever moves in the paths of the sea.

10   *O Lord our governor, ***
     how glorious is your name in all the world!

An alternative translation of verses 5–7

5   What are mortals, that you should be mindful of them? *
     mere human beings, that you should care for them?

6   You have made them little lower than the angels, *
     and crown them with glory and honour.

7   You have given them dominion over the works of your hands; *
     and put all things under their feet,

PSALM 9

1   I will give thanks to you, O Lord, with my whole heart; *
     I will tell of all your marvellous works.

2   I will be glad and rejoice in you; *
     I will make music to your name, O Most High.

3   When my enemies are driven back, *
     they stumble and perish at your presence.

4   For you have maintained my right and my cause; *
     you sat on your throne and gave righteous judgement.

5   You have rebuked the nations and destroyed the wicked; *
     you have blotted out their name for ever and ever.

6   The enemy was utterly laid waste, *
     you uprooted cities; even their memory has perished;

7   But the Lord shall endure for ever; *
     he has made fast his throne for judgement.

8   For he shall rule the world with righteousness; *
     and govern the peoples with equity.

9   Then will the Lord be a refuge for the oppressed, *
     a refuge in time of trouble.

10   And those who know your name will put their trust in you, *
     for you, Lord, have never failed those who seek you.

11   Sing praises to the Lord who dwells in Zion; *
     declare among the peoples the things he has done.

12   The avenger of blood has remembered them; *
     he did not forget the cry of the oppressed.

13   Have mercy upon me, O Lord; *
     consider the trouble I suffer from those who hate me,
        you that lift me up from the gates of death;

14   That I may tell all your praises in the gates of the city of Zion *
     and rejoice in your salvation.

15   The nations shall sink into the pit of their making, *
     and in the snare which they set will their own foot be taken.

16   The Lord makes himself known by his acts of justice; *
     the wicked are snared in the works of their own hands.

17   They shall return to the land of darkness; *
     all the nations that forget God.

18   For the needy shall not always be forgotten, *
     and the hope of the poor shall not perish for ever.

19   Rise up, O Lord; let not mortals have the upper hand; *
     let the nations be judged before your face.

20   Put them in fear, O Lord; *
     that the nations may know themselves to be but mortal.

PSALM 10

1   Why stand so far off, O Lord, *
    and hide yourself in time of trouble?

2   The wicked in their pride persecute the poor; *
    let them be caught in the schemes they have devised.

3   The wicked boast of their heart's desire; *
    the covetous curse and revile the Lord.

4   The wicked are so proud that they care not for God; *
    in all their scheming God counts for nothing.

5   They are brazen in all their ways,
        for your judgements are far above out of their sight; *
    they scoff at all their adversaries.

6   They say in their heart, 'I shall not be shaken; *
    no harm shall ever happen to me.'

7   Their mouth is full of cursing, deceit and fraud; *
    under their tongue lie mischief and wrong.

8   They lurk in the outskirts
        and in dark alleys they murder the innocent; *
    their eyes are ever watching for the helpless.

9   They lie in wait, like a lion in his den;
        they lie in wait to seize the poor; *
    they seize the poor when they get them into their net.

10 The innocent are broken and humbled before them; *
    the helpless fall before their power.

11 They say in their heart, 'God has forgotten; *
    he hides his face away; he will never see it.'

12 Arise, O Lord God, and lift up your hand; *
    forget not the poor.

13 Why should the wicked be scornful of God? *
    Why should they say in their hearts, 'You will not avenge it'?

14   Surely, you behold trouble and misery; *
     you see it and take it into your own hand.

15   The helpless commit themselves to you, *
     for you are the helper of the fatherless.

16   Break the power of the wicked and malicious; *
     search out their wickedness until you find none.

17   The Lord shall reign for ever and ever; *
     the nations shall perish from his land.

18   Lord, you will hear the desire of the poor; *
     you will incline your ear to the fullness of their heart;

19   To give justice to the orphan and oppressed, *
     so that mere flesh and blood may strike terror no more.

PSALM 11

1   In the Lord I take refuge; *
     how then can you say to me,
       'Flee like a bird to the hilltops?

2   'For see how the wicked bend the bow
       and fit their arrows to the string, *
     to shoot from the shadows at the true of heart.

3   'When the foundations are destroyed, *
     what can the righteous do?'

4   The Lord is in his holy temple; *
     the Lord's throne is in heaven.

5   His eyes behold, *
     his eyelids try the children of earth.

6   The Lord tries the righteous as well as the wicked, *
     but those who delight in violence his soul abhors.

7   Upon the wicked he shall rain coals of fire
         and burning sulphur; *
     scorching wind shall be their portion to drink.

8   For the Lord is righteous;
         he loves righteous deeds; *
     and those who are true shall see his face.

PSALM 12

1   Help, Lord, for there is no godly one left; *
     the faithful have vanished from among the children of earth.

2   They all speak falsely with their neighbour; *
     they flatter with their lips, but speak from a double heart.

3   O that the Lord would cut off all flattering lips, *
     and the tongue that speaks proud boasts!

4   Those who say, 'With our tongue will we prevail; *
     our lips are our own; who is lord over us?'

5   'Because of the oppression of the needy,
         and the groaning of the poor, *
     I will rise up now', says the Lord,
         'and set the hunted in safety.'

6   The words of the Lord are pure words, *
     like silver refined in the furnace
         and purified seven times in the fire.

7   You, O Lord, will watch over us *
     and guard us from this generation for ever.

8   The wicked strut on every side, *
     when what is vile is exalted by the children of earth.

PSALM 13

1   How long will you forget me, O Lord; for ever? *
     How long will you hide your face from me?

2   How long shall I have anguish in my soul,
       and grief in my heart, day after day? *
     How long shall my enemy triumph over me?

3   Look upon me and answer, O Lord my God; *
     lighten my eyes, lest I sleep in death;

4   Lest my enemy say, 'I have prevailed against you', *
     and my foes rejoice that I have fallen.

5   But I put my trust in your steadfast love; *
     my heart will rejoice in your salvation.

6   I will sing to the Lord, *
     for he has dealt so graciously with me.

PSALM 14

1   The fool has said in his heart, 'There is no God.' *
     Corrupt are they, and abominable in their wickedness;
       there is no one that does good.

2   The Lord has looked down from heaven upon the children
       of earth, *
     to see if there is any who is wise,
       and seeks after God.

3   But every one has turned back;
       all alike have become corrupt; *
     there is none that does good; no, not one.

4   Have they no knowledge, those evildoers, *
     who eat up my people as if they ate bread
       and do not call upon the Lord?

5   There shall they be brought in great fear; *
     for God is in the company of the righteous.

6   Though they would confound the counsels of the poor, *
     yet the Lord shall be their refuge.

7   O that Israel's salvation would come out of Zion! *
     When the Lord restores the fortunes of his people,
       then will Jacob rejoice and Israel be glad.

PSALM 15

1   Lord, who may dwell in your tabernacle? *
     Who may rest upon your holy hill?

2   Whoever leads an uncorrupt life, *
     does the thing that is right;

3   Who speaks the truth from the heart, *
     and bears no slander on the tongue;

4   Who does no evil to a friend; *
     and does not slander a neighbour;

5   In whose sight the wicked are not esteemed, *
     but who honours those who fear the Lord.

6   Whoever has sworn to a neighbour *
     and never goes back on that word;

7   Who does not lend money in hope of gain, *
     nor takes a bribe against the innocent;

8   Whoever does these things *
     shall never fall.

PSALM 16

1   Preserve me, O God, for in you have I taken refuge; *
I have said to the Lord, 'You are my God,
   my good above all other.'

2   All my delight is upon the godly that are in the land, *
upon those who are noble in heart.

3   But those who run after other gods *
shall have great trouble.

4   Their drink-offerings of blood will I not offer, *
neither make mention of their names upon my lips.

5   The Lord himself is my portion and my cup; *
in your hands alone is my fortune.

6   My share has fallen in a fair land; *
indeed, I have a goodly heritage.

7   I will bless the Lord who has given me counsel; *
and in the night watches he instructs my heart.

8   I have set the Lord always before me; *
he is at my right hand; I shall not fall.

9   Wherefore my heart is glad and my spirit rejoices; *
my body also shall rest in hope.

10   For you will not abandon my soul in death, *
nor suffer your faithful one to see the Pit.

11   You will show me the path of life;
   in your presence is the fullness of joy, *
and in your right hand are pleasures for evermore.

PSALM 17

1   Hear my just cause, O Lord; consider my complaint; *
      listen to my prayer, which comes not from lying lips.

2   Let my vindication come forth from your presence; *
      let your eyes behold what is right.

3   Weigh my heart, examine me by night; *
      refine me, and you will find no impurity in me.

4   My mouth does not trespass for earthly rewards; *
      I have heeded the words of your lips.

5   My footsteps hold fast in the ways of your commandments; *
      my feet have not stumbled in your paths.

6   I call upon you, O God, for you will answer me; *
      incline your ear to me, and listen to my words.

7   Show me your marvellous loving-kindness, *
      O Saviour of those who seek refuge
         from the rebels at your right hand.

8   Keep me as the apple of your eye; *
      hide me under the shadow of your wings,

9   From the wicked who assault me, *
      from my enemies who surround me to take away my life.

10   They have closed their heart to pity, *
      and their mouth speaks proud things.

11   They press me hard, they surround me on every side, *
      watching how they may cast me to the ground,

12   Like a lion, greedy for its prey, *
      like a young lion lurking in secret places.

13   Arise, O Lord; confront them and cast them down; *
      deliver me from the wicked by your sword.

14   Deliver me, O Lord, by your hand *
      from those whose portion in life is unending,

15   Whose bellies you fill with your treasure, *
      who are well supplied with children
          and leave their wealth to their little ones.

16   As for me, I shall see your face in righteousness; *
      when I awake and behold your likeness, I shall be satisfied.

PSALM 18

1   I love you, O Lord my strength, *
      The Lord is my crag, my fortress and my deliverer,

2   My God, my rock in whom I take refuge, *
      my shield, the horn of my salvation and my stronghold.

3   I cried to the Lord in my anguish, *
      and I was saved from my enemies.

4   The cords of death entwined me, *
      and the torrents of destruction overwhelmed me.

5   The cords of the Pit fastened about me, *
      and the snares of death entangled me.

6   In my distress I called upon the Lord *
      and cried out to my God for help.

7   He heard my voice in his temple; *
      and my cry came to his ears.

8   The earth trembled and quaked; *
      the foundations of the mountains shook;
          they reeled because he was angry.

9   Smoke rose from his nostrils
          and a consuming fire went out of his mouth; *
      burning coals blazed forth from him.

10   He parted the heavens and came down *
      and thick darkness was under his feet.

11 He rode upon the cherubim and flew; *
    he came flying on the wings of the wind.

12 He made darkness his covering round about him; *
    dark waters and thick clouds his pavilion.

13 From the brightness of his presence, through the clouds *
    burst hailstones and coals of fire.

14 The Lord also thundered out of heaven; *
    the Most High uttered his voice
        with hailstones and coals of fire.

15 He sent out his arrows and scattered them; *
    he hurled down lightnings and put them to flight.

16 The springs of the ocean were seen,
        and the foundations of the world uncovered, *
    at your rebuke, O Lord,
        at the blast of the breath of your displeasure.

17 He reached down from on high and took me; *
    he drew me out of the mighty waters.

18 He delivered me from my cruel enemy, *
    from foes that were too strong for me.

19 They came upon me in the day of my trouble; *
    but the Lord was my upholder.

20 He brought me out into a place of liberty; *
    he rescued me because he delighted in me.

21 The Lord rewarded me after my righteous dealing; *
    according to the cleanness of my hands he recompensed me,

22 Because I had kept the ways of the Lord *
    and had not gone wickedly away from my God;

23 For I had an eye to all his laws, *
    and did not cast out his commandments from me.

24 I was also whole-hearted before him *
and kept myself from iniquity;

25 Therefore the Lord rewarded me
after my righteous dealing, *
and according to the cleanness of my hands in his sight.

26 With the faithful you show yourself faithful; *
with the true you show yourself true.

27 With the pure you show yourself pure, *
but with the crooked you show yourself perverse.

28 For you will save a lowly people, *
and bring down the high looks of the proud.

29 You also shall light my candle; *
the Lord my God shall make my darkness to be bright.

30 By your help I shall run at an enemy host; *
with the help of my God I can leap over a wall.

31 As for God, his way is perfect;
the word of the Lord is tried in the fire; *
he is a shield to all who trust in him.

32 For who is God, but the Lord? *
and who is the rock, except our God?

33 It is God who girds me about with strength *
and makes my way perfect.

34 He makes my feet like hinds' feet *
so that I tread surely on the heights.

35 He teaches my hands to fight *
and my arms to bend a bow of bronze.

36 You have given me the shield of your salvation; *
your right hand upholds me,
and your grace has made me great.

37 You enlarge my strides beneath me, *
yet my footsteps do not slide.

38 I will pursue my enemies and overtake them, *
    nor turn again until I have destroyed them.

39 I will smite them down so they cannot rise; *
    they shall fall beneath my feet.

40 You have girded me with strength for the battle; *
    you will cast down my enemies under me;

41 You will make my foes turn their backs upon me *
    and I shall destroy all those that hate me.

42 They will cry out, but there shall be none to help them; *
    they will cry to the Lord, but he will not answer.

43 I shall beat them as small as the dust on the wind; *
    I will cast them out as the mire in the streets.

44 You will deliver me from the strife of the peoples; *
    you will make me the head of the nations.

45 A people I have not known shall serve me;
        as soon as they hear me, they shall obey me; *
    strangers will humble themselves before me.

46 The foreign peoples will lose heart; *
    and come trembling out of their strongholds.

47 The Lord lives, and blessèd be my rock! *
    Praised be the God of my salvation!

48 Even the God who vindicates me *
    and subdues the peoples under me.

49 You that deliver me from my enemies;
        you will set me up above my foes; *
    from the violent you will deliver me;

50 Therefore will I give you thanks, O Lord, among the nations, *
    and sing praises to your name;

51 To the one who gives salvation to his king; *
    and shows faithful love to his anointed,
        to David and his seed for ever.

PSALM 19

1   The heavens are telling the glory of God, *
     and the firmament proclaims his handiwork.

2   One day pours out its song to the next, *
     and one night unfolds knowledge to another.

3   They have neither speech nor language, *
     and their voices are not heard,

4   Yet their sound has gone out into all lands, *
     and their words to the ends of the world.

5   In them has he set a tabernacle for the sun *
     that comes forth as a bridegroom out of his chamber;
      and rejoices as a champion to run his course.

6   It goes forth from the end of the heavens
      and runs about to the very end again; *
     and there is nothing hidden from its heat.

7   The law of the Lord is perfect, reviving the soul; *
     the testimony of the Lord is sure
      and gives wisdom to the simple.

8   The statutes of the Lord are right and rejoice the heart; *
     the commandment of the Lord is pure
      and gives light to the eyes.

9   The fear of the Lord is clean and endures for ever; *
     the judgements of the Lord are true
      and righteous altogether.

10   More to be desired are they than gold,
      more than much fine gold, *
    sweeter also than honey,
      dripping from the honey-comb.

11   By them also is your servant enlightened, *
     and in keeping them there is great reward.

12   Who can tell how often they offend? *
       O cleanse me from my secret faults!

13   Keep your servant also from presumptuous sins
        lest they get dominion over me; *
       so shall I be undefiled,
        and innocent of great offence.

14   Let the words of my mouth and the meditation of my heart
        be acceptable in your sight, *
       O Lord, my strength and my redeemer.

PSALM 20

1   May the Lord hear you in the day of trouble, *
       the name of the God of Jacob defend you;

2   Send you help from his sanctuary *
       and strengthen you out of Zion;

3   Remember all your offerings *
       and accept your burnt sacrifice;

4   Grant you your heart's desire *
       and fulfil all your mind.

5   May we rejoice in your salvation
        and triumph in the name of our God; *
       may the Lord perform all your petitions.

6   Now I know that the Lord will save his anointed; *
       he will answer him from his holy heaven,
        with the mighty strength of his right hand.

7   Some put their trust in chariots and some in horses, *
       but we will call only on the name of the Lord our God.

8   They are brought down and fallen, *
       but we are risen and stand upright.

9   O Lord, save the king *
       and answer us when we call upon you.

PSALM 21

1 The king shall rejoice in your strength, O Lord; *
   how greatly shall he rejoice in your salvation!

2 You have given him his heart's desire; *
   and have not denied him the request of his lips.

3 For you come to meet him with blessings of goodness, *
   and set a crown of pure gold upon his head.

4 He asked of you life and you gave it to him; *
   length of days, for ever and ever.

5 His honour is great because of your salvation; *
   glory and majesty have you laid upon him.

6 You have granted him everlasting felicity *
   and will make him glad with joy in your presence.

7 For the king puts his trust in the Lord; *
   because of the loving-kindness of the Most High,
      he shall not be overthrown.

8 Your hand shall mark down all your enemies; *
   your right hand will find out those who hate you.

9 You will make them like a fiery oven
      in the time of your wrath; *
   the Lord will swallow them up in his anger
      and the fire shall consume them.

10 Their fruit you shall root out of the land *
   and their seed from among the children of earth.

11 Though they intend evil against you
      and devise wicked schemes, *
   yet shall they not prevail.

12 For you will put them to flight *
   when you aim at them on the bowstring.

13 Be exalted, O Lord, in your own might; *
   so will we make music and sing of your power.

PSALM 22

1   My God, my God, why have you forsaken me? *
and are so far from my cry
    and from the words of my distress?

2   O my God, I cry in the daytime,
    but you do not answer; *
and by night, but I find no rest.

3   Yet you are the Holy One, *
enthroned upon the praises of Israel.

4   Our forebears trusted in you; *
they trusted, and you delivered them.

5   They cried out to you and were delivered; *
they put their trust in you and were not confounded.

6   But as for me, I am a worm and no man, *
scorned by all and despised by the people.

7   All who see me laugh me to scorn; *
they curl their lips and wag their heads, saying,

8   'He trusted in the Lord; let him deliver him; *
let him deliver him, if he delights in him.'

9   But you are he who took me out of the womb, *
and laid me safe upon my mother's breasts.

10   On you was I cast ever since I was born; *
you are my God even from my mother's womb.

11   Be not far from me, for trouble is near at hand, *
and there is none to help.

12   Mighty oxen come around me; *
fat bulls of Bashan close me in on every side.

13   They gape upon me with their mouth, *
as it were a ramping and a roaring lion.

14   I am poured out like water;
        all my bones are out of joint; *
    my heart has become like wax
        melting in the depths of my body.

15   My mouth is dried up like a pot-sherd;
        my tongue cleaves to my gums; *
    you have laid me in the dust of death.

16   For the hounds are all about me,
        the pack of evildoers close in on me; *
    they pierce my hands and my feet.

17   I can count all my bones; *
    they stand staring and looking upon me.

18   They divide my garments among them; *
    they cast lots for my clothing.

19   Be not far from me, O Lord; *
    you are my strength; hasten to help me.

20   Deliver my soul from the sword, *
    my poor life from the power of the dog.

21   Save me from the lion's mouth, *
    from the horns of wild oxen – you will answer me!

22   I will tell of your name to my people; *
    in the midst of the congregation will I praise you.

23   Praise the Lord, you that fear him; *
    O seed of Jacob, glorify him;
        stand in awe of him, O seed of Israel.

24   For he has not despised nor abhorred the suffering of the poor;
        neither has he hidden his face from them; *
    but when he cried to him he heard him.

25   From you comes my praise in the great congregation; *
    I will perform my vows
        in the presence of those that fear you.

26 The poor shall eat and be satisfied; *
    those who seek the Lord shall praise him;
        their hearts shall live for ever.

27 All the ends of the earth
        shall remember and turn to the Lord, *
    and all the families of the nations shall bow before him.

28 For the kingdom is the Lord's; *
    and he rules over the nations.

29 How can those who sleep in the earth
        bow down in worship; *
    all who go down to the dust kneel before him?

30 My soul shall live for him;
        my descendants shall serve him; *
    this shall be told of the Lord for generations to come.

31 They shall come and make known to a people yet unborn *
    that he, the Lord, has done it.

PSALM 23

1 The Lord is my shepherd; *
    therefore can I lack nothing.

2 He makes me lie down in green pastures *
    and leads me beside still waters.

3 He shall refresh my soul *
    and guide me in the paths of righteousness for his name's sake.

4 Even though I walk through the valley of the shadow of death,
        I will fear no evil; *
    for you are with me;
        your rod and your staff, they comfort me.

5 You have spread a table before me
        in the presence of those who trouble me; *
    you have anointed my head with oil
        and my cup shall be full.

6   Surely, goodness and loving mercy shall follow me
       all the days of my life *
    and I will dwell in the house of the Lord for ever.

PSALM 24

1   The earth is the Lord's and all its fullness, *
    the compass of the world and all who dwell therein.

2   For he has founded it upon the seas *
    and set it firm upon the rivers of the deep.

3   'Who shall ascend the hill of the Lord? *
    or who can rise up in his holy place?'

4   'Those who have clean hands and are pure in heart, *
    who have not lifted up their soul to vanity,
       nor sworn an oath to deceive;

5   'They shall receive a blessing from the Lord, *
    a just reward from God their saviour.'

6   Such is the company of those who seek him, *
    who seek your face, O God of Jacob.

7   Lift up your heads, O gates;
       and be lifted up, you everlasting doors; *
    and the King of glory shall come in.

8   'Who is the King of glory?' *
    'The Lord, strong and mighty,
       the Lord who is mighty in battle.'

9   Lift up your heads, O gates;
       and be lifted up, you everlasting doors; *
    and the King of glory shall come in.

10   'Who is this King of glory?' *
    'The Lord of hosts,
       he is the King of glory.'

PSALM 25

1   To you, O Lord, I lift up my soul;
      O my God, in you I trust; *
    let me not be put to shame;
      let not my enemies triumph over me.

2   Let none who look to you be put to shame; *
    let the treacherous rather be shamed and frustrated.

3   Make me to know your ways, O Lord, *
    and teach me your paths.

4   Lead me in your truth and teach me, *
    for you are the God of my salvation;
      for you have I hoped all the day long.

5   Remember, O Lord, your compassion and love, *
    for they are from everlasting.

6   Remember not the sins of my youth
      or my transgressions; *
    but according to your steadfast love
      think upon me, O Lord, in your goodness.

7   Gracious and upright is the Lord; *
    therefore shall he teach sinners in his way.

8   He will guide the humble in doing right *
    and teach his way to the lowly.

9   All the paths of the Lord are mercy and truth *
    to those who keep his covenant and his testimonies.

10   For your name's sake, O Lord, *
    be merciful to my sin, for it is great.

11   Who are those who fear the Lord? *
    Them will he teach in the way that they should choose.

12   Their soul shall dwell at ease, *
    and their offspring shall inherit the land.

13 The friendship of the Lord is for those who fear him *
and he will show them his covenant.

14 My eyes are ever looking to the Lord, *
for he shall pluck my feet out of the net.

15 Turn to me and be gracious to me, *
for I am alone and brought very low.

16 The sorrows of my heart have increased; *
O bring me out of my distress.

17 Look upon my adversity and misery *
and forgive me all my sin.

18 Look upon my enemies, for they are many, *
and they bear a violent hatred against me.

19 O keep my soul and deliver me; *
let me not be put to shame, for I have put my trust in you.

20 Let integrity and uprightness preserve me, *
for my hope has been in you.

21 Deliver Israel, O God, *
out of all his troubles.

PSALM 26

1 Give judgement for me, O Lord,
    for I have walked with integrity; *
I have trusted in the Lord and have not faltered.

2 Test me, O Lord, and try me; *
examine my heart and my mind.

3 For your love is before my eyes; *
I have walked in your truth.

4 I have not joined the company of the false, *
nor consorted with the deceitful.

5   I hate the gathering of evildoers; *
    and I will not sit down with the wicked.

6   I will wash my hands in innocence, O Lord, *
    that I may go about your altar,

7   To make the voice of thanksgiving heard *
    and tell of all your wonderful deeds.

8   Lord, I love the house of your habitation *
    and the place where your glory abides.

9   O sweep me not away with sinners, *
    nor my life with the bloodthirsty,

10 Whose hands are full of wicked schemes, *
    and their right hand full of bribes.

11 As for me, I will walk with integrity; *
    redeem me, O Lord, and be merciful to me.

12 My foot stands firm; *
    in the great congregation I will bless the Lord.

PSALM 27

1   The Lord is my light and my salvation;
        whom then shall I fear? *
    The Lord is the strength of my life;
        of whom then shall I be afraid?

2   When the wicked came upon me to eat up my flesh, *
    these my enemies and my foes stumbled and fell.

3   Though a host encamp against me,
        my heart shall not be afraid; *
    and though there rose up war against me,
        yet will I put my trust in him.

4   One thing have I asked of the Lord;
        and that alone I seek; *
    that I may dwell in the house of the Lord
        all the days of my life;

5   To behold the fair beauty of the Lord *
    and to learn his will in his temple.

6   For in the day of trouble
        he shall hide me in his shelter; *
    in the secret place of his dwelling shall he hide me
        and set me high upon a rock.

7   And now shall he lift up my head *
    above my enemies round about me;

8   Therefore will I offer in his dwelling an oblation
        with great gladness; *
    I will sing and make music to the Lord.

9   Hearken to my voice, O Lord, when I call; *
    have mercy upon me and answer me.

10 My heart tells of your word, 'Seek my face.' *
    Your face, Lord, will I seek.

11 Hide not your face from me, *
    nor cast your servant away in displeasure.

12 You have been my helper; *
    leave me not, neither forsake me, O God of my salvation.

13 Though my father and my mother forsake me, *
    the Lord will take me up.

14 Teach me your way, O Lord; *
    lead me on a level path,
        because of those who lie in wait for me.

15 Deliver me not into the will of my adversaries, *
    for false witnesses have risen up against me,
        and those who breathe out violence.

16 I believe that I shall see the goodness of the Lord *
    in the land of the living.

17 Wait for the Lord;
        be strong and he shall comfort your heart; *
    wait patiently for the Lord.

PSALM 28

1   Unto you I call, O Lord my rock,
      be not deaf to my cry; *
    lest, if you do not hear me,
      I become like those who go down to the Pit.

2   Hear the voice of my prayer when I cry out to you, *
    when I lift up my hands to your holy of holies.

3   Do not snatch me away with the wicked,
      with the evildoers, *
    who speak peaceably with their neighbours,
      while strife is in their hearts.

4   Repay them according to their deeds, *
    and according to the wickedness of their devices.

5   Reward them according to the work of their hands, *
    and pay them their just deserts.

6   They take no heed of the Lord's doings,
      nor of the works of his hands; *
    therefore shall he break them down
      and not build them up.

7   Blessèd be the Lord! *
    for he has heard the voice of my prayer.

8   The Lord is my strength and my shield; *
    my heart has trusted in him and I am helped;

9   Therefore my heart dances for joy, *
    and in my song will I praise him.

10 The Lord is the strength of his people, *
    a safe refuge for his Anointed.

11 Save your people and bless your inheritance; *
    shepherd them and carry them for ever.

PSALM 29

1   Ascribe to the Lord, you powers of heaven, *
    ascribe to the Lord glory and strength.

2   Ascribe to the Lord the honour due to his name; *
    worship the Lord in the beauty of holiness.

3   The voice of the Lord is upon the waters;
        the God of glory thunders; *
    the Lord is upon the mighty waters.

4   The voice of the Lord is mighty in operation; *
    the voice of the Lord is a glorious voice.

5   The voice of the Lord breaks the cedar trees; *
    the Lord breaks the cedars of Lebanon;

6   He makes Lebanon skip like a calf, *
    and Sirion like a young wild ox.

7   The voice of the Lord splits the flash of lightning;
        the voice of the Lord shakes the wilderness; *
    the Lord shakes the wilderness of Kadesh.

8   The voice of the Lord makes the oak trees writhe
        and strips the forests bare; *
    in his temple all cry, 'Glory!'

9   The Lord sits enthroned above the waterflood; *
    the Lord sits enthroned as king for evermore.

10 The Lord shall give strength to his people; *
    the Lord shall give his people the blessing of peace.

PSALM 30

1   I will exalt you, O Lord,
        because you have lifted me up *
    and have not let my foes triumph over me.

2   O Lord my God, I cried out to you, *
    and you have healed me.

3   You brought me up, O Lord, from the dead; *
    you restored me to life from among those that go down to the Pit.

4   Sing to the Lord, you servants of his; *
    give thanks to his holy name.

5   For his wrath endures but the twinkling of an eye,
        his favour for a lifetime. *
    Heaviness may endure for the night,
        but joy comes in the morning.

6   In my prosperity I said,
        'I shall never be moved. *
    You, Lord, of your goodness,
        have made my hill so strong.'

7   Then you hid your face from me, *
    and I was utterly dismayed.

8   To you, O Lord, I cried; *
    to the Lord I made my supplication:

9   'What profit is there in my blood,
        if I go down to the Pit? *
    Will the dust praise you or declare your faithfulness?

10 'Hear, O Lord, and have mercy upon me; *
    O Lord, be my helper.'

11 You have turned my mourning into dancing; *
    you have put off my sack-cloth and girded me with gladness;

12 Therefore my heart sings to you without ceasing; *
    O Lord my God, I will give you thanks for ever.

PSALM 31

1   In you, O Lord, have I taken refuge;
        let me never be put to shame; *
    deliver me in your righteousness.

2   Incline your ear to me; *
    make haste to deliver me.

3   Be my strong rock, a fortress to save me,
        for you are my rock and my stronghold; *
    guide me, and lead me for your name's sake.

4   Take me out of the net
        that they have laid secretly for me, *
    for you are my strength.

5   Into your hands I commend my spirit, *
    for you have redeemed me, O Lord God of truth.

6   I hate those who cling to worthless idols; *
    I put my trust in the Lord.

7   I will be glad and rejoice in your mercy; *
    for you have seen my affliction;
        and known my soul in adversity.

8   You have not shut me up in the hand of the enemy; *
    you have set my feet in an open place.

9   Have mercy on me, O Lord, for I am in trouble; *
    my eye is consumed with sorrow;
        my soul and my body also.

10   For my life is wasted with grief,
        and my years with sighing; *
    my strength fails me because of my affliction,
        and my bones are consumed.

11   I have become a reproach to all my enemies
        and even to my neighbours,
        an object of dread to my acquaintances; *
    when they see me in the street they flee from me.

12   I am forgotten like one that is dead, out of mind; *
    I have become like a broken vessel.

13   For I have heard the whispering of the crowd;
        fear is on every side; *
    they scheme together against me,
        and plot to take my life.

14   But my trust is in you, O Lord. *
     I have said, 'You are my God.

15   'My times are in your hand; *
     deliver me from the hand of my enemies,
          and from those who persecute me.

16   'Make your face to shine upon your servant, *
     and save me for your mercy's sake.'

17   Lord, let me not be confounded
          for I have called upon you; *
     rather, let the wicked be put to shame;
          let them be silent in the grave.

18   Let the lying lips be put to silence *
     that speak against the righteous
          with arrogance, disdain and contempt.

19   How abundant is your goodness, O Lord,
          which you have laid up for those who fear you; *
     which you have prepared in the sight of all
          for those who put their trust in you.

20   You hide them in the shelter of your presence
          from those who slander them; *
     you keep them safe in your shelter from the strife of tongues.

21   Blessèd be the Lord! *
     for he has shown me the wonders of his love
          besieged in a city.

22   I had said in my alarm,
          'I have been cut off from the sight of your eyes.' *
     Nevertheless, you heard the voice of my prayer
          when I cried out to you.

23   Love the Lord, all you his servants; *
     for the Lord protects the faithful,
          but repays to the full the proud.

24   Be strong and let your heart take courage, *
     all you who wait in hope for in the Lord.

PSALM 32

1   Happy is the one whose transgression is forgiven, *
    and whose sin is covered!

2   Happy is the one to whom the Lord imputes no guilt, *
    and in whose spirit there is no guile!

3   While I held my tongue, my bones wasted away *
    through my groaning all day long.

4   For your hand was heavy upon me day and night; *
    my moisture was dried up like the drought in summer.

5   Then I acknowledged my sin to you, *
    and my iniquity I did not hide.

6   I said, 'I will confess my transgressions to the Lord': *
    and you forgave the guilt of my sin;

7   Therefore let all the faithful make their prayers to you
       in time of trouble; *
    in the great water-flood, it shall not reach them.

8   You are a place for me to hide in;
       you preserve me from trouble; *
    you surround me with songs of deliverance.

9   'I will instruct you and teach you
       in the way that you should go; *
    I will guide you with my eye.

10   'Be not like horse or mule which have no understanding; *
    whose mouths must be held with bit and bridle,
       else they will not stay near you.'

11   Great tribulations remain of the wicked; *
    but mercy embraces those who trust in the Lord.

12   Be glad, you righteous, and rejoice in the Lord; *
    shout for joy, all who are true of heart.

PSALM 33

1   Rejoice in the Lord, O you righteous; *
for it is good for the just to sing praises.

2   Praise the Lord with the harp; *
on the ten-stringed lyre sing his praise.

3   Sing for him a new song; *
play skilfully with shouts of praise.

4   For the word of the Lord is true, *
and all his works are sure.

5   He loves righteousness and justice; *
the earth is full of the loving-kindness of the Lord.

6   By the word of the Lord were the heavens made, *
and all their host by the breath of his mouth.

7   He gathers up the waters of the sea as in a water-skin *
and lays up the deep in his treasury.

8   Let all the earth fear the Lord; *
stand in awe of him, all who dwell in the world.

9   For he spoke, and it was done; *
he commanded, and it stood fast.

10   The Lord brings the counsel of the nations to naught; *
he frustrates the designs of the peoples.

11   But the counsel of the Lord shall endure for ever, *
and the designs of his heart from generation to generation.

12   Happy the nation whose God is the Lord! *
and the people he has chosen for his own!

13   The Lord looks down from heaven, *
and beholds all the children of earth.

14   From where he sits enthroned he turns his gaze *
on all who dwell on the earth.

15 He fashions all the hearts of them *
    and understands all their works.

16 No king is saved by the might of his host; *
    no warrior delivered by his great strength.

17 A horse is a vain hope for deliverance; *
    for all its strength it cannot save.

18 Behold, the eye of the Lord
        is upon those who fear him, *
    on those who wait in hope for his steadfast love,

19 To deliver their soul from death, *
    and to feed them in time of famine.

20 Our soul waits longingly for the Lord; *
    he is our help and our shield.

21 Indeed, our heart rejoices in him; *
    in his holy name have we put our trust.

22 Let your loving-kindness, O Lord, be upon us, *
    as we have set our hope on you.

PSALM 34

1   I will bless the Lord at all times; *
    his praise shall ever be in my mouth.

2   My soul shall glory in the Lord; *
    let the humble hear and be glad.

3   O magnify the Lord with me; *
    let us exalt his name together.

4   I sought the Lord and he answered me *
    and delivered me from all my fears.

5   Look upon him and be radiant, *
    and your faces shall not be ashamed.

6   This poor soul cried, and the Lord heard me *
      and saved me from all my troubles.

7   The angel of the Lord
         encamps around those who fear him, *
      and delivers them.

8   O taste and see that the Lord is gracious; *
      happy the one who trusts in him!

9   Fear the Lord, all you his holy ones, *
      for those who fear him lack nothing.

10   Lions may lack and suffer hunger, *
      but those who seek the Lord
         lack nothing that is good.

11   Come, my children, and listen to me; *
      I will teach you the fear of the Lord.

12   Who among you delights in life *
      and longs for days to enjoy good things?

13   Keep your tongue from evil *
      and your lips from lying words.

14   Turn from evil and do good; *
      seek peace and pursue it.

15   The eyes of the Lord are upon the righteous, *
      and his ears are open to their cry.

16   The face of the Lord is against those who do evil, *
      to root out the remembrance of them from the earth.

17   The righteous cry and the Lord hears them *
      and delivers them out of all their troubles.

18   The Lord is near to the brokenhearted *
      and will save those who are crushed in spirit.

19   Many are the troubles of the righteous, *
      but the Lord will deliver them out of all.

20 He keeps all their bones; *
    so that not one of them is broken.

21 But evil shall slay the wicked, *
    and those who hate the righteous will be condemned.

22 The Lord ransoms the life of his servants, *
    and none who seek refuge in him shall be condemned.

PSALM 35

1 Contend, O Lord, with those that contend with me; *
    fight against those that fight against me.

2 Take up shield and buckler *
    and rise up to help me.

3 Take up the spear and bar the way
    against those who pursue me; *
    say to my soul, 'I am your salvation.'

4 Let those who seek after my life be shamed and disgraced; *
    let those who plot my ruin fall back and be put to confusion.

5 Let them be as chaff before the wind; *
    with angel of the Lord scattering them.

6 Let their way be dark and slippery, *
    with the angel of the Lord pursuing them.

7 For they have secretly spread a net for me without a cause; *
    without any cause have they dug a pit for my soul.

8 Let ruin come upon them unawares; *
    let them be caught in the net they laid;
      let them fall to destruction in it.

9 Then will my soul be joyful in the Lord; *
    and glory in his salvation.

10 My very bones will say, 'Lord, who is like you? *
    You deliver the poor from those that are too strong for them,
      the poor and needy from those who would despoil them.'

11 False witnesses rose up against me; *
    they charged me with things I knew not.

12 They rewarded me evil for good; *
    to the desolation of my soul.

13 But as for me, when they were sick I put on sack-cloth *
    and humbled myself with fasting;

14 When my prayer returned empty to my bosom, *
    it was as though I grieved for my friend or brother; *

15 I behaved as one who mourns for his mother, *
    bowed down and brought very low.

16 But when I stumbled, they gathered in delight;
    they gathered together against me; *
    as if they were strangers I did not know
    they tore at me without ceasing.

17 When I fell they mocked me; *
    they gnashed at me with their teeth.

18 O Lord, how long will you look on? *
    Rescue my soul from their ravages,
    and my poor life from the young lions.

19 I will give you thanks in the great congregation; *
    I will praise you in the mighty throng.

20 Do not let my treacherous foes rejoice over me, *
    let them not wink who hate me without a cause.

21 For they do not speak of peace, *
    but invent deceitful schemes against those that are quiet in the land.

22 They opened wide their mouths at me and said, *
    'Aha! Aha! we saw it with our very eyes.'

23 This you have seen, O Lord; do not keep silent; *
    go not far from me, O Lord.

24 Awake, arise, to my cause! *
    To my defence, my God and my Lord!

25 Give me justice, O Lord my God,
        according to your righteousness; *
    let them not triumph over me.

26 Let them not say to themselves,
        'Aha! we have our heart's desire' *
    let them not say, 'We have swallowed you up.'

27 Let all who rejoice at my trouble be put to shame and confusion; *
    let those who boast against me
        be clothed with shame and dishonour.

28 Let those who favour my cause rejoice and be glad; *
    let them say always,
        'Great is the Lord, who delights in his servant's well-being.'

29 So shall my tongue be talking of your righteousness *
    and of your praise all the day long.

PSALM 36

1   Sin whispers to the wicked, in the depths of their heart; *
    there is no fear of God before their eyes.

2   They flatter themselves in their own eyes *
    that their abominable sin will not be found out.

3   The words of their mouth are unrighteous and full of deceit; *
    they have ceased to act wisely and ceased to do good.

4   They think out mischief upon their beds
        and have set themselves in no good way; *
    nor do they abhor that which is evil.

5   Your love, O Lord, reaches to the heavens, *
    and your faithfulness to the clouds.

6   Your righteousness stands like the strong mountains,
        your justice like the great deep; *
    you, Lord, shall save both man and beast.

7   How precious is your loving mercy, O God! *
    the children of earth shall take refuge
        under the shadow of your wings.

8   They shall be satisfied with the abundance of your house; *
    they shall drink from the river of your delights.

9   For with you is the well of life, *
    and in your light shall we see light.

10 O continue your loving-kindness to those who know you, *
    and your righteousness to those who are true of heart.

11 Let not the foot of pride come against me, *
    nor the hand of the ungodly thrust me down.

12 See how they are fallen, all who work wickedness! *
    they are cast down and shall not be able to stand.

PSALM 37

1   Do not fret because of evildoers; *
    do not be jealous of those who do wrong.

2   For they shall soon wither like grass, *
    and like the green herb fade away.

3   Trust in the Lord and be doing good; *
    dwell in the land and be nourished with truth.

4   Let your delight be in the Lord, *
    and he will give you your heart's desire.

5   Commit your way to the Lord
        and put your trust in him, *
    and he will bring it to pass.

6   He will make your righteousness as clear as the light *
    and your just dealing as the noonday.

7   Be still before the Lord and wait for him; *
      do not fret over those that prosper,
         as they follow these evil schemes.

8   Leave off from wrath and let go displeasure; *
      do not fret, lest you be moved to do evil.

9   For evildoers shall be cut off, *
      but those who wait upon the Lord shall possess the land.

10   Yet a little while and the wicked shall be no more; *
      you will search for their place and find them gone.

11   But the lowly shall possess the land; *
      and shall delight in abundance of peace.

12   The wicked plot against the righteous *
      and gnash at them with their teeth.

13   The Lord shall laugh at the wicked, *
      for he sees that their day is coming.

14   The wicked draw their sword and bend their bow
         to strike down the poor and needy, *
      to slaughter those who walk in truth.

15   Their sword shall go through their own heart, *
      and their bow shall be broken.

16   The little that the righteous have *
      is better than great riches of the wicked.

17   For the arms of the wicked shall be broken, *
      but the Lord upholds the righteous.

18   The Lord knows the days of the godly, *
      and their inheritance shall stand for ever.

19   They shall not be put to shame in the perilous time, *
      and in days of famine they shall have enough.

20   But the wicked shall perish,
         and the enemies of the Lord, like the glory of the meadows,
      shall vanish; *
      they shall vanish like smoke.

21   The wicked borrow and do not repay, *
       but the righteous are generous in giving.

22   For those who are blessed by God shall possess the land, *
       but those who are cursed by him shall be rooted out.

23   When your steps are guided by the Lord; *
       and you delight in his way,

24   Though you stumble, you shall not fall headlong, *
       for the Lord holds you fast by the hand.

25   I have been young and now I am old, *
       yet never have I seen the righteous forsaken,
          or their children begging their bread.

26   All the day long they are generous in lending, *
       and their children also shall be blessed.

27   Depart from evil and do good, *
       and you shall abide for ever.

28   For the Lord loves the thing that is right; *
       and will not forsake his faithful ones.

29   They shall be kept safe for ever, *
       but the offspring of the wicked shall be rooted out.

30   The righteous shall possess the land *
       and dwell in it for ever.

31   The mouth of the righteous utters wisdom, *
       and their tongue speaks the thing that is right.

32   The law of their God is in their heart, *
       and their footsteps shall not slide.

33   The wicked spy on the righteous *
       and seek occasion to slay them.

34   The Lord will not leave them in their hand, *
       nor let them be condemned when they are judged.

35   Wait upon the Lord and keep his way; *
       he will raise you up to possess the land,
          and when the wicked are uprooted, you shall see it.

36   I myself have seen the wicked in great power, *
       and flourishing like a green bay tree.

37   I went by and lo, they were gone; *
       I sought them, but they could nowhere be found.

38   Keep innocence and heed the thing that is right; *
       for that will bring you peace at the last.

39   But the sinners shall perish together; *
       and the posterity of the wicked shall be rooted out.

40   The salvation of the righteous comes from the Lord; *
       he is their stronghold in the time of trouble.

41   The Lord shall stand by them and save them; *
       he shall deliver them from the wicked and shall save them,
         because they have put their trust in him.

PSALM 38

1   Rebuke me not, O Lord, in your anger; *
       nor chasten me in your heavy displeasure.

2   For your arrows have stuck fast in me, *
       and your hand presses hard upon me.

3   There is no health in my flesh,
         because of your indignation; *
       there is no peace in my bones, because of my sin.

4   For my iniquities have gone over my head; *
       their weight is a burden too heavy to bear.

5   My wounds stink and fester *
       because of my foolishness.

6   I am utterly bowed down and brought very low; *
       I go about mourning all the day long.

7 My loins are filled with searing pain; *
 there is no whole part in my body.

8 I am feeble and utterly broken; *
 I roar aloud, because of the disquiet of my heart.

9 O Lord, you know all my desires, *
 and my sighing is not hidden from you.

10 My heart is pounding, my strength has failed me, *
 the light of my eyes is gone from me.

11 My friends and companions stand apart from my affliction; *
 my neighbours stand afar off.

12 Those who seek after my life lay snares for me; *
 and those who would harm me whisper evil
  and mutter slander all the day long.

13 But I am like one who is deaf and who hears not, *
 like one that is dumb, who does not open his mouth.

14 I have become like one who does not hear *
 and from whose mouth comes no retort.

15 For in you, O Lord, have I put my trust; *
 you will answer me, O Lord my God.

16 For I prayed, 'Let them not triumph over me, *
 those who exult over me when my foot slips.'

17 Truly, I am on the verge of falling, *
 and my pain is ever with me.

18 I will confess my iniquity *
 and be sorry for my sin.

19 Those that are my enemies without any cause are mighty, *
 and those who hate me wrongfully are many in number.

20 Those who repay evil for good are against me, *
 because I follow after the good.

21   Forsake me not, O Lord; *
       be not far from me, O my God.

22   Make haste to help me, *
       O Lord God of my salvation.

PSALM 39

1   I said, 'I will keep watch over my ways, *
       so that I offend not with my tongue.

2   'I will guard my mouth with a muzzle *
       while the wicked are in my sight.'

3   So I held my tongue and said nothing; *
       I kept silent, to no avail.

4   My distress increased, my heart grew hot within me; *
       while I mused, the fire was kindled; *
         and I spoke out with my tongue:

5   'Lord, let me know my end and the number of my days, *
       that I may know how short my time is.

6   'You have made my days as it were a handspan,
         and my lifetime is as nothing in your sight; *
       truly, even those who stand upright are but a breath.

7   'We walk about like a shadow
         and in vain we are in turmoil; *
       we heap up riches and cannot tell who will gather them.

8   'And now, what is my hope? *
       Truly my hope is even in you.

9   'Deliver me from all my transgressions *
       and do not make me the taunt of the fool.'

10   I fell silent and did not open my mouth, *
       for surely it was your doing.

11   Take away your plague from me; *
     I am consumed by the blows of your hand.

12   With rebukes for sin you punish us;
        like a moth you consume our beauty; *
     truly, everyone is but a breath.

13   Hear my prayer, O Lord, and give ear to my cry; *
     hold not your peace at my tears.

14   For I am but a stranger with you, *
     a passing alien, as all my forebears were.

15   Turn your gaze from me, that I may be glad again, *
     before I go my way and am no more.

PSALM 40

1   I waited patiently for the Lord; *
     he inclined to me and heard my cry.

2   He brought me out of the seething pit,
        out of the mire and clay; *
     he set my feet upon a rock and made my footing sure.

3   He has put a new song in my mouth,
        a song of praise to our God; *
     many shall see and fear
        and put their trust in the Lord.

4   Happy the one who trusts in the Lord! *
     who does not turn to the proud that follow a lie.

5   Great are the wonders you have done, O Lord my God!
        How great your designs for us! *
     There is none that can be compared with you.

6   If I were to proclaim them and tell of them *
     they would be more than I were able to express.

7   Sacrifice and offering you do not desire *
     but my ears you have opened;

8   Burnt-offering and sacrifice for sin you have not required, *
    then said I: 'Lo, I come.

9   'In the scroll of the book it is written of me
        that I should do your will, O my God; *
    I delight to do it: your law is within my heart.'

10 I have declared your righteousness in the great congregation; *
    behold, I did not restrain my lips;
        and that, O Lord, you know.

11 Your righteousness have I not hidden in my heart;
        I have spoken of your faithfulness and your salvation; *
    I have not concealed your loving kindness and truth
        from the great congregation.

12 Do not withhold your compassion from me, O Lord; *
    let your love and your faithfulness always preserve me,

13 For innumerable troubles have come about me;
        my sins have overtaken me so that I cannot look up; *
    they are more in number than the hairs of my head,
        and my heart fails me.

14 Be pleased, O Lord, to deliver me; *
    O Lord, make haste to help me.

15 Let them be ashamed and altogether dismayed
        who seek after my life to destroy it; *
    let them be driven back and put to shame
        who wish me evil.

16 Let them be desolate because of their shame, *
    those who say to me, 'Aha, Aha!'

17 Let all who seek you rejoice in you and be glad; *
    let those who love your salvation say continually,
        'Great is the Lord!'

18 Though I am poor and needy, *
    the Lord cares for me.

19 You are my helper and my deliverer; *
    O my God, make no delay.

PSALM 41

1   Blessed are those who consider the poor and needy! *
The Lord will deliver them in the time of trouble.

2   The Lord preserves them and restores their life,
      that they may be happy in the land; *
he will not hand them over to the will of their enemies.

3   The Lord sustains them on their sick-bed *
you, Lord, remake their bed in their sickness.

4   And so I pray, 'Lord, be merciful to me; *
heal me, for I have sinned against you.'

5   My enemies speak evil about me: *
'When will he die and his name perish?'

6   If they come to see me, they utter empty words; *
their heart gathers mischief;
      when they go out, they tell it abroad.

7   All my enemies whisper together against me *
against me they devise this evil.

8   'A deadly thing has laid hold on him; *
he will not rise again from where he lies.'

9   Even my bosom friend, whom I trusted,
      who ate of my bread, *
has lifted up his heel against me.

10   But you, O Lord, be merciful to me *
and raise me up, that I may reward them.

11   By this I know that you favour me, *
that my enemy does not triumph over me.

12   Because of my integrity, you uphold me, *
and shall set me before your face for ever.

13   Blessèd be the Lord God of Israel, *
from everlasting to everlasting. Amen and Amen.

PSALM 42

1   As the deer longs for the water-brooks, *
    so longs my soul for you, O God.

2   My soul is athirst for God, for the living God; *
    when shall I come to behold the face of God?

3   My tears have been my food day and night, *
    while all day long they say to me, 'Where is now your God?'

4   Now when I think on these things, I pour out my soul: *
    how I went with the multitude
        and led the procession to the house of God,

5   With the voice of praise and thanksgiving, *
    among those who kept holy-day.

· 6   *Why are you so full of heaviness, O my soul? *
    and why are you so disquieted within me?*

7   *O put your trust in God; *
    for I will yet give him thanks,
        who is the help of my countenance, and my God.*

8   My soul is heavy within me; *
    therefore I will remember you from the land of Jordan,
        and from Hermon and the hill of Mizar.

9   Deep calls to deep in the thunder of your waterfalls; *
    all your waves and billows have gone over me.

10   The Lord will grant his loving-kindness in the daytime; *
    through the night his song will be with me,
        a prayer to the God of my life.

11   I say to God my rock,
        'Why have you forgotten me? *
    and why go I so heavily, while the enemy oppresses me?'

12   As though they would crush my very bones,
        my enemies mock me; *
    while they say to me all the day long,
        'Where now is your God?'

13   *Why are you so full of heaviness, O my soul?* *
     and why are you so disquieted within me?

14   *O put your trust in God;* *
     for I will yet give him thanks,
       who is the help of my countenance, and my God.

PSALM 43

1   Give judgement for me, O God,
       and defend my cause against an ungodly people; *
     O deliver me from the deceitful and the wicked.

2   For you are the God of my refuge;
       why have you cast me from you? *
     and why go I so heavily, while the enemy oppresses me?

3   O send out your light and your truth, that they may lead me, *
     and bring me to your holy hill and to your dwelling;

4   That I may go to the altar of God,
       to the God of my joy and gladness; *
     and on the harp I will give thanks to you, O God my God.

5   *Why are you so full of heaviness, O my soul?* *
     and why are you so disquieted within me?

6   *O put your trust in God;* *
     for I will yet give him thanks,
       who is the help of my countenance, and my God.

PSALM 44

1   We have heard with our ears, O God, our fathers have told us, *
     all that you did in their days, in the time of old.

2   How with your hand you drove out nations and planted us in; *
     and broke the power of peoples and set us free.

3   For not by their own sword did our fathers take the land, *
     nor did their own arm save them;

4   But your right hand, your arm, and the light of your countenance, *
because you were gracious to them.

5   You are my King and my God *
who commanded salvation for Jacob.

6   Through you we drove back our adversaries; *
through your name we tread down our foes.

7   For I did not trust in my bow, *
it was not my own sword that saved me;

8   It was you that saved us from our enemies *
and put our adversaries to shame.

9   We gloried in God all the day long, *
and were ever praising your name.

10   But now you have rejected and brought us to shame *
and go not forth with our armies.

11   You have made us turn our backs on our enemies, *
and our enemies have despoiled us.

12   You have made us like sheep to be slaughtered *
and have scattered us among the nations.

13   You have sold your people for a pittance *
and made no profit on their sale.

14   You have made us the taunt of our neighbours, *
the scorn and derision of those that are round about us.

15   You have made us a byword among the nations, *
among the peoples they wag their heads.

16   My confusion is daily before me, *
and the shame of my face has covered me;

17   At the taunts of the slanderer and reviler, *
at the sight of the enemy and avenger.

18   All this has come upon us,
       though we have not forgotten you, *
    and have not played false to your covenant.

19   Our hearts have not turned back, *
    nor our steps gone out of your way,

20   Yet you have crushed us in the place of dragons, *
    and covered us with the shadow of death.

21   If we have forgotten the name of our God, *
    or stretched out our hands to any strange god,

22   Will not God search it out? *
    For he knows the secrets of the heart.

23   But for your sake are we killed all the day long; *
    and are counted as sheep for the slaughter.

24   Rise up! Why sleep, O Lord? *
    Awake, and do not reject us for ever.

25   Why do you hide your face *
    and forget our grief and oppression?

26   Our soul is bowed down to the dust; *
    our belly cleaves to the earth.

27   Rise up O Lord, and help us, *
    and redeem us for the sake of your steadfast love.

PSALM 45

1   My heart is overflowing with a word of grace; *
    as I make my song for the king,
       my tongue is the pen of a ready writer.

2   You are fairer than all; *
    full of grace are your lips,
       for God has blessed you for ever.

3   Gird your sword upon your thigh, O mighty one, *
    gird on your majesty and glory.

4   Ride on and prosper in the cause of truth *
    and for the sake of humility and righteousness.

5   Your right hand will teach you terrible things; *
        your arrows shall be sharp in the heart of the king's enemies,
    so that peoples fall under you.

6   Your throne is God's throne, for ever, *
    the sceptre of your kingdom is the sceptre of righteousness;

7   You love righteousness and hate iniquity; *
    therefore God, your God, has anointed you
        with the oil of gladness above your fellows.

8   Your garments are fragrant with myrrh, aloes and cassia, *
    from ivory palaces the music of strings makes you glad.

9   Kings' daughters are among your honourable women; *
    at your right hand stands the queen in gold of Ophir.

10 'Hear, O daughter; consider and incline your ear; *
    forget your own people and your father's house.

11 'So shall the king have pleasure in your beauty; *
    he is your lord, so do him honour.

12 'The people of Tyre shall bring you gifts; *
    the richest of the people shall seek your favour.'

13 The king's daughter is all glorious within; *
    her clothing is embroidered cloth-of-gold.

14 She shall be brought to the king in raiment of needlework; *
    the virgins that follow her shall also be led to you.

15 With joy and gladness shall they be brought, *
    and enter into the palace of the king.

16 'Instead of your fathers you shall have sons; *
    whom you shall make princes over all the earth.

17   'I will make your name to be remembered
        through all generations; *
    therefore shall the peoples praise you for ever and ever.'

PSALM 46

1   God is our refuge and strength, *
    a very present help in trouble;

2   Therefore we will not fear, though the earth be moved, *
    and though the mountains tremble in the heart of the sea;

3   Though the waters rage and swell *
    and though the mountains quake at the towering seas:

4   *The Lord of hosts is with us; *
    the God of Jacob is our stronghold.*

5   There is a river whose streams make glad the city of God, *
    the holy place of the dwelling of the Most High.

6   God is in the midst of her;
        therefore shall she not be removed; *
    God shall help her at the break of day.

7   The nations are in uproar and the kingdoms are shaken; *
    but God utters his voice and the earth shall melt away.

8   *The Lord of hosts is with us; *
    the God of Jacob is our stronghold.*

9   Come and behold the works of the Lord, *
    what destruction he has wrought upon the earth.

10   He makes wars to cease in all the world; *
    he breaks the bow and snaps the spear
        and burns the chariots in the fire.

11   'Be still, and know that I am God; *
    I will be exalted among the nations;
        I will be exalted in the earth.'

12   *The Lord of hosts is with us; *
    the God of Jacob is our stronghold.*

PSALM 47

1   Clap your hands together, all you peoples; *
    O sing unto God with shouts of joy.

2   For the Lord Most High is to be feared; *
    he is the great King over all the earth.

3   He subdued the peoples under us, *
    and the nations under our feet.

4   He has chosen our heritage for us, *
    the pride of Jacob, whom he loves.

5   God has gone up with a merry noise, *
    the Lord with the sound of the trumpet.

6   O sing praises to God, sing praises; *
    sing praises to our King, sing praises.

7   For God is the King of all the earth; *
    sing praises with all your skill.

8   God reigns over the nations; *
    God has taken his seat upon his holy throne.

9   The nobles of the peoples are gathered together *
    with the people of the God of Abraham.

10 For the shields of the earth now belong to God, *
    and he is very highly exalted.

PSALM 48

1   Great is the Lord and highly to be praised; *
    in the city of our God.

2   His holy mountain is fair and lifted high, *
    the joy of all the earth;

3   On Mount Zion, the heavenly mountain, *
    stands the city of the great king.

4   In her citadels God has shown himself *
    to be a tower of refuge.

5   For behold, the kings of the earth assembled *
    and swept forward together.

6   They saw, and were dumbfounded; *
    dismayed, they fled in terror.

7   Trembling seized them there;
        they writhed like a woman in labour, *
    as when the east wind shatters the ships of Tarshish.

8   As we had heard, so have we seen
        in the city of the Lord of hosts, the city of our God: *
    God has established her for ever.

9   We have waited on your loving-kindness, O God, *
    in the midst of your temple.

10 Like your name, O God,
        so your praise reaches to the ends of the earth; *
    your right hand is full of righteousness.

11 Let Mount Zion rejoice and the daughters of Judah be glad, *
    because of your judgements, O Lord.

12 Walk about Sion and go round about her;
        count all her towers; *
    consider well her bulwarks; pass through her citadels,

13 That you may tell those who come after
        that such is our God for ever and ever. *
    It is he that shall be our guide for evermore.

PSALM 49

1   Hear this, all you peoples; *
     listen, all you that dwell in the world,

2   You of low or high degree, *
     both rich and poor together.

3   My mouth shall speak of wisdom, *
     and my heart shall meditate on understanding.

4   I will incline my ear to a parable; *
     I will unfold my riddle with the harp.

5   Why should I fear in evil days, *
     when the malice of my foes surrounds me,

6   Such as trust in their goods, *
     and glory in the abundance of their riches?

7   For no one can at the last be ransomed, *
     or pay to God the price of deliverance.

8   To ransom a soul is too costly, *
     there is no price one could pay for it,

9   So that they might live for ever, *
     and never see the grave.

10   For we see that the wise die also;
        with the foolish and ignorant they perish *
     and leave their riches to others.

11   Their tomb is their home for ever,
        their dwelling through all generations, *
     though they call their lands after their own names.

12   Mortals cannot abide in their honour; *
     they are like the beasts that perish.

13   Such is the way of those who boast in themselves, *
     the end of those who delight in their own words.

14 Like a flock of sheep they are destined to die;
  death is their shepherd; *
  they go down straight to the Pit.

15 Their beauty shall waste away, *
  and the land of the dead shall be their dwelling.

16 But God shall ransom my soul; *
  from the grasp of death will he take me.

17 Be not envious if some grow rich *
  and the glory of their house increases,

18 For they will carry nothing away when they die, *
  nor will their glory follow after them.

19 Though they count themselves happy while they live, *
  and praise you for your success,

20 They shall enter the company of those gone before them, *
  who will nevermore see the light.

21 A mortal in honour, but with no understanding, *
  is like the beasts that perish.

PSALM 50

1 The Lord, the most mighty God, has spoken *
  and called the world from the rising of the sun to its setting.

2 Out of Zion, perfect in beauty, God shines forth; *
  our God comes and will not keep silence. *

3 Consuming fire goes out before him, *
  and a mighty tempest stirs about him.

4 He calls the heaven above, *
  and the earth, that he may judge his people.

5 'Gather to me my faithful, *
  who have sealed my covenant with sacrifice.'

6   Let the heavens declare his righteousness; *
       for he is the God of justice.

7   Hear, O my people, and I will speak: *
       'I will testify against you, O Israel;
          for I am God, your God.

8   'I will not reprove you for your sacrifices and burnt-offerings *
       for they are always before me.

9   'I will take no bullock out of your house, *
       nor he-goat out of your folds;

10   'For all the beasts of the forest are mine, *
       the cattle upon a thousand hills.

11   'I know every bird of the mountains, *
       and every creature of the field is in my sight.

12   'If I were hungry, I would not tell you, *
       for the whole world is mine and all that fills it.

13   'Do you think I eat the flesh of bulls, *
       or drink the blood of goats?

14   'Offer to God a sacrifice of thanksgiving *
       and fulfil your vow to God Most High.

15   'Call upon me in the day of trouble; *
       I will deliver you and you shall honour me.'

16   But to the wicked, says God: *
       'Why do you recite my statutes
          and take my covenant upon your lips,

17   'Since you refuse to be disciplined, *
       and have cast my words behind you?

18   'When you saw a thief, you made friends with him, *
       and you threw in your lot with adulterers.

19 'You have loosed your lips for evil, *
and harnessed your tongue to deceit.

20 'You sit and speak evil of your brother *
you slander your own mother's son.

21 'These things have you done, and should I keep silence? *
Did you think that I am even such a one as yourself?

22 'But no, I must reprove you; *
and set before your eyes the things that you have done.

23 'You that forget God, consider this well, *
lest I tear you apart and there is none to deliver you.

24 'Whoever offers me the sacrifice of thanksgiving honours me; *
but to those who keep my way
will I show the salvation of God.'

PSALM 51

1 Have mercy on me, O God, in your great goodness; *
according to the abundance of your compassion
blot out my offences.

2 Wash me thoroughly from my wickedness *
and cleanse me from my sin.

3 For I acknowledge my faults *
and my sin is ever before me.

4 Against you only have I sinned *
and done what is evil in your sight;

5 So that you are justified in your sentence *
and righteous in your judgement.

6 I have been wicked from my very birth, *
a sinner even when my mother conceived me.

7 Behold, you desire truth deep within me *
and shall make me understand wisdom in the depths of my heart.

8 Purge me with hyssop and I shall be clean; *
  wash me and I shall be whiter than snow.

9 Make me hear of joy and gladness *
  that the bones you have broken may rejoice.

10 Turn your face from my sins *
  and blot out all my misdeeds.

11 Make me a clean heart, O God, *
  and renew a right spirit within me.

12 Cast me not away from your presence *
  and take not your holy spirit from me.

13 Give me again the joy of your salvation *
  and sustain me with your gracious spirit;

14 Then shall I teach your ways to the wicked *
  and sinners shall return to you.

15 Deliver me from my guilt, O God,
   the God of my salvation, *
  and my tongue shall sing of your righteousness.

16 O Lord, open my lips, *
  and my mouth shall proclaim your praise.

17 For you desire no sacrifice, else I would give it; *
  you take no delight in burnt-offerings.

18 The sacrifice of God is a broken spirit; *
  a broken and contrite heart, O God, you will not despise.

19 O be favourable and gracious to Zion; *
  build up the walls of Jerusalem.

20 Then you will accept sacrifices offered in righteousness,
   the burnt-offerings and oblations; *
  then shall they offer up bulls on your altar.

PSALM 52

1   Why do you glory in evil, you tyrant, *
    while the goodness of God endures continually?

2   You plot destruction, you deceiver; *
    your tongue is like a sharpened razor.

3   You love evil rather than good, *
    falsehood rather than the word of truth.

4   You love all words that hurt, *
    O you deceitful tongue.

5   Therefore God shall utterly bring you down; *
    he shall take you and pluck you out of your tent
        and root you out of the land of the living.

6   The righteous shall see this and tremble, *
    they shall laugh you to scorn, and say:

7   'This is the one who did not take God for a refuge, *
    but trusted in great riches and relied upon wickedness.'

8   But I am like a green olive tree in the house of God; *
    I trust in the goodness of God for ever and ever.

9   I will always give thanks to you for what you have done *
    and before your faithful
        will I declare how gracious is your name.

PSALM 53

1   Fools say in their heart, 'There is no God.' *
    Corrupt are they, and abominable in their wickedness;
        there is none that does good.

2   God has looked down from heaven upon the children of earth *
    to see if there is any who is wise and seeks after God.

3   They are all gone out of the way;
        all alike have become corrupt; *
    there is none that does good, no not one.

4   Have they no knowledge, those evildoers, *
       who eat up my people as though they eat bread,
          and do not call upon God?

5   They shall fear, with such fear as never was; *
       for God will scatter the bones of the ungodly.

6   They will be put to shame, *
       because God has rejected them.

7   O that Israel's salvation would come out of Zion! *
       When God restores the fortunes of his people
          then will Jacob rejoice and Israel be glad.

PSALM 54

1   Save me, O God, by your name; *
       and vindicate me by your power.

2   Hear my prayer, O God; *
       give heed to the words of my mouth.

3   For strangers have risen up against me,
          and the ruthless seek after my soul; *
       they have not set God before them.

4   Behold, God is my helper; *
       the Lord is he that upholds my soul.

5   May evil rebound on those who lie in wait for me; *
       destroy them in your faithfulness.

6   An offering of a free heart will I give you *
       and praise your name, O Lord, for it is gracious.

7   For he has delivered me out of all my trouble, *
       and my eye shall see the downfall of my enemies.

PSALM 55

1   Hear my prayer, O God; *
     hide not yourself from my petition.

2   Give heed to me and answer me; *
     I am restless in my complaining.

3   I am alarmed at the voice of the enemy *
     and at the clamour of the wicked;

4   For they would bring down evil upon me *
     and are set against me in fury.

5   My heart is disquieted within me, *
     and the terrors of death have fallen upon me.

6   Fearfulness and trembling are come upon me, *
     and a horrible dread has overwhelmed me.

7   And I said: 'O that I had wings like a dove *
     for then would I fly away and be at rest.

8   'Then would I flee away far off *
     and make my lodging in the wilderness.

9   'I would make haste to escape *
     from the stormy wind and tempest.'

10   Confuse their tongues, O Lord, and divide them; *
     for I have seen violence and strife in the city.

11   Day and night they go about on her walls, *
     and in her midst stalk mischief and trouble.

12   Wickedness walks in her streets; *
     deceit and guile never leave her squares.

13   For it was not an open enemy that reviled me, *
     for then I could have borne it;

14   Nor was it my adversary that puffed himself up against me, *
     for then I would have hid myself from him.

15 But it was even you, one like myself, *
my companion and my own familiar friend.

16 We took sweet counsel together, *
and walked in the house of God as friends.

17 Let death come suddenly upon them;
let them go down alive to the Pit; *
for wickedness inhabits their dwellings, their very hearts.

18 As for me, I will call upon God, *
and the Lord will deliver me.

19 In the evening and morning and at noonday
I will pray and make my supplication; *
and he shall hear my voice.

20 He shall redeem my soul in peace
from the battle waged against me; *
for many have come upon me.

21 God, who is enthroned of old,
will hear and bring them down; *
for they will not repent, and they have no fear of God.

22 My companion stretched out his hands against his friend; *
and has broken his covenant;

23 His speech was softer than butter, though war was in his heart; *
his words were smoother than oil, but are naked swords.

24 Cast your burden upon the Lord and he will sustain you; *
and will not let the righteous fall for ever.

25 But those that are bloodthirsty and deceitful, O God *
you will bring down to the pit of destruction.

26 They shall not live out half their days; *
but my trust shall be in you, O Lord.

PSALM 56

1   Have mercy on me, O God, for they trample over me; *
    all day long they assault and oppress me.

2   My adversaries trample over me all the day long; *
    many are they that fight against me, O Most High.

3   And yet in the day of my fear, *
    I put my trust in you.

4   In God, whose word I praise,
        in God I trust, and will not fear, *
    for what can flesh do to me?

5   All day long they wound me with words; *
    their every thought is to do me evil.

6   They band together and lie in wait; *
    marking my steps, they seek my life.

7   Shall they escape for all their wickedness? *
    In anger, O God, cast the peoples down.

8   You have counted all my groans;
        put my tears into your bottle; *
    are they not noted in your book?

9   Then shall my enemies turn back
        on the day when I call upon you, *
    this I know, for God is on my side.

10 In God whose word I praise,
        in God I trust and will not fear; *
    what can flesh do to me?

11 To you, O God, will I fulfil my vows; *
    to you will I present my offerings of thanks;

12 For you will deliver my soul from death
        and my feet from falling, *
    that I may walk before God in the light of the living.

PSALM 57

1   Be merciful to me, O God, be merciful to me, *
     for my soul takes refuge in you;

2   In the shadow of your wings will I take refuge *
     until the storm of destruction has passed by.

3   I will call upon the Most High God, *
     to the God who fulfils his purpose for me.

4   He will send from heaven and save me
     and rebuke those that would trample upon me; *
    God will send forth his love and his faithfulness.

5   I lie in the midst of fiery lions, *
     whose teeth are spears and arrows,
     and their tongue a sharp sword.

6   *Exalt yourself, O God, above the heavens, *
    and your glory over all the earth.*

7   They have laid a net for my feet
     my soul is pressed down; *
    they have dug a pit before me
     and will fall into it themselves.

8   My heart is ready, O God, my heart is ready; *
     I will sing and give you praise.

9   Awake, my soul; awake, lyre and harp *
     that I may awaken the dawn.

10   I will give you thanks, O Lord, among the peoples; *
     I will sing praise to you among the nations.

11   For your loving-kindness reaches to the heavens, *
     and your truth unto the clouds.

12   *Be exalted, O God, above the heavens, *
    and your glory over all the earth.*

PSALM 58

1   Do you indeed speak justly, O you mighty? *
     Do you rule the peoples with equity?

2   With unjust heart you act throughout the land, *
     you deal out the violence of your hands.

3   The wicked are estranged from the womb; *
     those who speak falsehood go astray from their birth.

4   They are as venomous as a serpent, *
     they are like the deaf adder which stops its ears,

5   Which does not heed the voice of the charmers, *
     and is deaf to the skilful weaver of spells.

6   Break, O God, their teeth in their mouths; *
     the fangs of these lions, O Lord, destroy.

7   Let them vanish like water that runs away; *
     let them have no strength to aim their shafts.

8   Let them be as the snail that melts into slime, *
     like one lost from the womb that never sees the sun.

9   Before ever their pots feel the heat of the thorns, *
     green or blazing, let them be swept away.

10   The righteous will be glad when they see God's vengeance; *
     they will bathe their feet in the blood of the wicked.

11   So that people will say,
      'Truly, there is a harvest for the righteous; *
     truly, there is a God who judges in the earth.'

PSALM 59

1   Rescue me from my enemies, O my God; *
    set me high above those that rise up against me.

2   O save me from the evil-doers *
    and from murderous foes deliver me.

3   For see how they lie in wait for my soul, *
    and the mighty gather together against me.

4   Not for any fault or sin of mine, O Lord; *
    for no offence, they run and prepare themselves for war.

5   Rouse yourself, come to my aid and see; *
    for you are the Lord of hosts, the God of Israel.

6   Awake, and judge all the nations; *
    show no mercy to the evil traitors.

7   They gather at night-fall and growl like dogs; *
    and prowl about the city.

8   They pour out evil words with their mouths;
        swords are on their lips; *
    'For who', they say, 'can hear us?'

9   But you laugh at them, O Lord; *
    you hold all the nations in derision.

10 For you, O my strength, will I watch; *
    for you, O God, are my strong tower.

11 My God in his steadfast love will come to me; *
    he will let me behold the downfall of my enemies.

12 Slay them not, lest my people forget; *
    send them reeling by your might
        and bring them down, O Lord our shield.

13 For the sins of their mouth, for the words of their lips, *
    let them be taken in their pride.

14   For the cursing and falsehood that they have uttered *
      consume them in wrath, consume them till they are no more.

15   And they shall know that God rules in Jacob, *
      and to the ends of the earth.

16   And still they gather at night-fall and growl like dogs; *
      and prowl about the city.

17   Though they forage for something to devour, *
      and howl if they are not filled,

18   Yet will I sing of your strength *
      and every morning praise your steadfast love;

19   For you have been my stronghold, *
      my refuge in the day of my trouble.

20   To you, O my strength, will I sing; *
      for you, O God, are my refuge,
        my God of steadfast love.

PSALM 60

1   O God, you have cast us off and scattered us; *
      you have been angry; O restore us to yourself again.

2   You have shaken the earth and torn it apart; *
      heal its wounds, for it trembles.

3   You have shown your people bitter things; *
      we reel from the deadly wine you have given us.

4   You have made those who fear you to flee, *
      to escape from the range of the bow.

5   Save us by your right hand, and answer us, *
      that your beloved may be delivered.

6   God has spoken from his holy place: *
      'I will triumph and divide Shechem,
        and share out the valley of Succoth.

7   'Gilead is mine and Manasseh is mine; *
      Ephraim is my helmet and Judah my sceptre.

8   'Moab shall be my wash-pot,
       over Edom will I cast my sandal, *
      across Philistia will I shout in triumph.'

9   Who will lead me into the strong city? *
      Who will bring me into Edom?

10   Have you not cast us off, O God? *
      Will you no longer go forth with our hosts?

11   O grant us your help against the enemy, *
      for earthly help is in vain.

12   Through God will we do great acts, *
      for it is he that shall tread down our enemies.

PSALM 61

1   Hear my crying, O God, *
      and listen to my prayer.

2   From the end of the earth I call to you with fainting heart; *
      O lead me to the rock that is higher than I.

3   For you are my refuge, *
      a strong tower against the enemy.

4   Let me dwell in your tent for ever; *
      and take refuge under the cover of your wings.

5   For you, O God, will hear my vows; *
      you will grant the desire of those who fear your name.

6   You will add length of days to the life of the king; *
      that his years may endure throughout all generations.

7   May he sit enthroned before God for ever; *
      bid steadfast love and truth watch over him.

8   So will I always sing the praise to your name, *
      and day by day fulfil my vows.

PSALM 62

1   In stillness waits my soul on God alone; *
     from him comes my salvation.

2   He alone is my rock and my salvation, *
     my stronghold, so that I shall not be greatly shaken.

3   How long will you all assail me, that you may destroy me, *
     as you would a tottering wall or a leaning fence?

4   They plot only to thrust me down from my place of honour,
        lies are their chief delight; *
     they bless with their mouth, but in their heart they curse.

5   In stillness wait on God, my soul; *
     in him alone is my hope.

6   He alone is my rock and my salvation, *
     my stronghold, so that I shall not be shaken.

7   In God is my strength and my glory; *
     God is my strong rock; in him is my refuge.

8   Put your trust in him always, my people, *
     pour out your hearts before him, for God is our refuge.

9   The peoples are but a breath;
        the children of earth deceive; *
     on the scales they are altogether lighter than air.

10   Put no trust in oppression; in robbery take no empty pride; *
     though wealth increase, set not your heart upon it.

11   God spoke once, and twice have I heard the same, *
     that power belongs to God.

12   Steadfast love belongs to you, O Lord, *
     for you repay everyone according to their deeds.

PSALM 63

1   O God, you are my God; eagerly I seek you; *
    my soul is athirst for you.

2   My flesh also faints for you, *
    as in a barren and dry land where there is no water.

3   So would I gaze upon you in your holy place, *
    that I might behold your power and your glory.

4   Your loving-kindness is better than life itself; *
    and so shall my lips praise you.

5   As long as I live will I bless you *
    and lift up my hands in your name.

6   My soul shall be satisfied, as with marrow and fatness, *
    and my mouth shall praise you with joyful lips,

7   When I remember you upon my bed, *
    and meditate on you in the watches of the night.

8   For you have been my helper, *
    and under the shadow of your wings will I rejoice.

9   My soul clings to you; *
    your right hand shall hold me fast.

10 But those who seek my soul to destroy it *
    shall go down into the depths of the earth;

11 Let them fall by the edge of the sword, *
    and become a portion for foxes.

12 But the king shall rejoice in God;
        all those who swear by him shall be glad, *
    for the mouth of those who speak lies shall be stopped.

PSALM 64

1   Hear my voice, O God, in my prayer; *
    preserve my life from fear of the enemy.

2   Hide me from the conspiracy of the wicked, *
    from the gathering of evildoers.

3   They sharpen their tongue like a sword, *
    and aim their bitter words like arrows,

4   That they may shoot down the blameless from ambush; *
    suddenly they shoot, and are not seen.

5   They hold fast to their evil course; *
    they talk of laying snares, saying 'Who will see us?'

6   They search out wickedness and lay a cunning trap, *
    for deep are the inward thoughts of the heart.

7   But God will shoot at them with his swift arrow *
    and suddenly they shall be wounded.

8   Their own tongues shall make them fall, *
    and all who see them shall wag their heads in scorn.

9   All peoples shall fear and tell what God has done; *
    and they will ponder all his works.

10 The righteous shall rejoice in the Lord
        and put their trust in him, *
    and all that are true of heart shall exult.

PSALM 65

1   Praise waits for you, O God, in Zion, *
    to you that answer prayer shall vows be paid.

2   To you shall all flesh come to confess their sins; *
    when our misdeeds prevail against us,
        you will purge them away.

3   Happy are they whom you choose
        and draw to your courts to dwell there! *
    We shall be satisfied with the blessings of your house,
        even of your holy temple.

4   Awesome things will you show us in your righteousness,
        O God of our salvation, *
    O hope of all the ends of the earth
        and of the farthest seas.

5   You in your strength set fast the mountains *
    and are girded about with might.

6   You stilled the raging of the seas, *
    the roaring of their waves,
        and the clamour of the peoples.

7   Those who dwell at the ends of the earth
        tremble at your marvels; *
    the gates of the morning and evening sing your praise.

8   You visit the earth and water it; *
    you make it very plenteous.

9   The river of God is full of water; *
    You prepare grain for your people,
        for so you provide.

10 You drench the furrows and smooth out the ridges; *
    you soften the ground with showers and bless its increase.

11 You crown the year with your goodness, *
    and your paths overflow with plenty.

12 May the pastures of the wilderness flow with goodness, *
    and the hills be girded with joy.

13 May the meadows be clothed with flocks of sheep; *
    and the valleys stand so thick with corn
        that they shall laugh and sing.

PSALM 66

1 O be joyful in God, all you lands; *
    sing to the honour of his name;
        make his praise glorious.

2 Say to God, 'How awesome are your deeds! *
    Because of your great strength
        your enemies shall bow before you.

3 'All the earth shall worship you, *
    sing to you, sing praise to your name.'

4 Come now and behold the works of God, *
    how wonderful he is in his dealings with the children of earth.

5 He turned the sea into dry land;
        the river also they went through on foot; *
    there we rejoiced in him.

6 In his might he rules for ever;
        his eyes keep watch over the nations; *
    let no rebel rise up against him.

7 Bless our God, O you peoples; *
    make the voice of his praise to be heard;

8 Who holds our souls in life, *
    and suffers not our feet to slip.

9 For you, O God, have proved us; *
    you have tried us as silver is tried.

10 You brought us into the snare; *
    you laid heavy burdens upon our backs.

11 You let enemies ride over our heads;
        we went through fire and water; *
    but you brought us out into a place of liberty.

12 I will come into your house with burnt-offerings
        and will pay you my vows, *
    which my lips uttered
        and my mouth promised when I was in trouble.

13 I will offer you fat burnt-sacrifices
        with the smoke of rams; *
    I will sacrifice oxen and goats.

14 Come and listen, all you who fear God, *
    and I will tell you what he has done for my soul.

15 I called out to him with my mouth, *
    and his praise was on my tongue.

16 If I had nursed evil in my heart, *
    the Lord would not have heard me;

17 But in truth God has heard me; *
    he has heeded the voice of my prayer.

18 Blessèd be God, who has not rejected my prayer, *
    nor withheld his loving mercy from me.

PSALM 67

1 God be merciful to us and bless us, *
   and make his face to shine upon us,

2 That your way may be known upon earth, *
   your saving power among all nations.

3 *Let the peoples praise you, O God; *
   let all the peoples praise you.*

4 O let the nations rejoice and be glad, *
   for you will judge the peoples righteously
       and govern the nations upon earth.

5 *Let the peoples praise you, O God; *
   let all the peoples praise you.*

6   Then shall the earth bring forth her increase; *
      and God, our own God, will give us his blessing.

7   May God give us his blessing, *
      and all the ends of the world will fear him.

PSALM 68

1   Let God arise and let his enemies be scattered; *
      let those that hate him flee before him.

2   As the smoke vanishes, so may they vanish away; *
      as wax melts at the fire,
        so let the wicked perish at the presence of God.

3   But let the righteous be glad and rejoice before God; *
      let them make merry with gladness.

4   Sing to God, sing praises to his name;
        exalt him who rides on the clouds; *
      The Lord is his name; rejoice before him!

5   Father of the fatherless, defender of widows, *
      God in his holy habitation!

6   God gives the solitary a home
        and brings forth prisoners to songs of welcome; *
      but the rebellious inhabit a burning desert.

7   O God, when you went forth before your people, *
      when you marched through the wilderness,

8   The earth shook and the heavens dropped down rain,
        at the presence of God, the Lord of Sinai, *
      at the presence of God, the God of Israel.

9   You sent down a gracious rain, O God; *
      you refreshed your inheritance when it was weary.

10   Your people came to dwell there; *
      in your goodness, O God, you provide for the poor.

11   The Lord gave the word;
         great was the company of women who bore the tidings: *
     'Kings and their armies they flee, they flee!'
         and women at home are dividing the spoil.

12   Though you stayed among the sheepfolds, *
     see now a dove's wings covered with silver,
         and its feathers with green gold.

13   When the Almighty scattered the kings, *
     it was like snow-flakes falling on Zalmon.

14   O mighty mountain, great mountain of Bashan! *
     O towering mountain, great mountain of Bashan!

15   Why look with envy, you towering mountain,
         at the hill which God has desired for his dwelling, *
     the place where the Lord will dwell for ever?

16   The chariots of God are twice ten thousand,
         even thousands upon thousands; *
     the Lord is among them, the Lord of Sinai in holy power.

17   You have gone up on high and led captivity captive; *
     you have received as tribute those who rebelled,
         that you may reign as Lord and God.

18   Blessèd be the Lord who bears our burdens day by day, *
     for God is our salvation.

19   God is for us the God of our salvation; *
     God is the Lord who can deliver us from death.

20   God will smite the head of his enemies, *
     the hairy scalp of those who walk in wickedness.

21   The Lord has said, 'From the heights of Bashan; *
     from the depths of the sea will I bring them back.

22   'Till you dip your foot in blood, *
     and the tongue of your dogs has a taste of your enemies.'

23 We see your solemn procession, O God, *
your procession into the sanctuary, my God and my King.

24 The singers go before, the musicians follow after, *
in the midst of maidens playing on timbrels.

25 In your companies, bless your God; *
bless the Lord, you that are of the fount of Israel.

26 At the head there is Benjamin, least of the tribes;
the princes of Judah in joyful company; *
the princes of Zebulon and Naphtali.

27 Send forth your strength, O God; *
establish, O God, what you have wrought in us.

28 For your temple's sake in Jerusalem *
kings shall bring their gifts to you.

29 Drive back with your word the wild beast of the reeds *
the herd of the bull-like, the brutish hordes.

30 Trample down those who lust after silver; *
scatter the peoples that delight in war.

31 Vessels of bronze shall be brought from Egypt; *
Ethiopia will stretch out her hands to God.

32 Sing to God, O kingdoms of the earth; *
make music in praise of the Lord;

33 He rides on the ancient heaven of heavens; *
and sends forth his voice, a mighty voice.

34 Give glory to God, whose splendour is over Israel; *
whose glory is above the clouds.

35 How terrible is God in his holy sanctuary, *
the God of Israel, who gives strength and power to his people!
Blessèd be God!

PSALM 69

1   Save me, O God, *
       for the waters have come up, even to my neck.

2   I sink in deep mire where there is no foothold; *
       I have come into deep waters and the flood sweeps over me.

3   I have grown weary with crying, my throat is raw; *
       my eyes have failed from looking so long for my God.

4   Those who hate me without any cause *
       are more than the hairs of my head;

5   Those who would destroy me are mighty; *
       my enemies accuse me falsely:
          must I now give back what I never stole?

6   O God, you know my foolishness, *
       and my faults are not hidden from you.

7   Let not those who hope in you
          be put to shame through me, Lord God of hosts; *
       let not those who seek you be disgraced because of me,
          O God of Israel.

8   For your sake have I suffered reproach, *
       shame has covered my face.

9   I have become a stranger to my kindred, *
       an alien to my mother's children.

10   Zeal for your house has eaten me up; *
       the scorn of those who scorn you has fallen upon me.

11   I humbled myself with fasting, *
       but that was turned to my reproach.

12   I put on sack-cloth also, *
       and became a byword among them.

13   Those who sit at the gate murmur against me, *
       and the drunkards make songs about me.

14 But as for me, I make my prayer to you, O Lord; *
 at an acceptable time, O God.

15 Answer me, O God, in the abundance of your mercy, *
 and with your sure salvation.

16 Draw me out of the mire, that I sink not; *
 let me be rescued from those who hate me
  and out of the deep waters.

17 Let not the water-flood drown me,
   neither the deep swallow me up; *
 let not the Pit shut its mouth upon me.

18 Answer me, O Lord, for your loving-kindness is good; *
 turn to me in the multitude of your mercies.

19 Hide not your face from your servant; *
 be swift to answer me, for I am in trouble.

20 Draw near to my soul and redeem me; *
 deliver me because of my enemies.

21 You know my reproach, my shame and my dishonour; *
 my adversaries are all in your sight.

22 Reproach has broken my heart; I am full of heaviness. *
 I looked for some to have pity, but there was no one,
  neither found I any to comfort me.

23 They gave me gall to eat, *
 and when I was thirsty, they gave me vinegar to drink.

24 Let the table before them be a trap *
 and their sacred feasts a snare.

25 Let their eyes be darkened, that they cannot see, *
 and give them continual trembling in their loins.

26 Pour out your indignation upon them, *
 and let the heat of your anger overtake them.

27 Let their camp be desolate, *
   and let there be no one to dwell in their tents.

28 For they persecute him whom you have stricken *
   and increase the sorrows of him whom you have pierced.

29 Lay to their charge guilt upon guilt, *
   and let them not receive your vindication.

30 Let them be wiped out of the book of the living *
   and not be written among the righteous.

31 As for me, I am poor and in misery; *
   your saving help, O God, will lift me up.

32 I will praise the name of God with a song; *
   I will proclaim his greatness with thanksgiving.

33 This will please the Lord more than an offering of oxen, *
   more than bullocks with horns and hoofs.

34 The humble shall see and be glad; *
   you who seek God, your heart shall live.

35 For the Lord listens to the needy, *
   and his own who are imprisoned he does not despise.

36 Let the heavens and the earth praise him, *
   the seas and all that moves in them;

37 For God will save Zion and rebuild the cities of Judah; *
   they shall live there and have it in possession.

38 The children of his servants shall inherit it, *
   and they that love his name shall dwell therein.

PSALM 70

1   O God, make speed to save me; *
     O Lord, make haste to help me.

2   Let those who seek my life
       be put to shame and confusion; *
     let them be turned back and disgraced
       who wish me evil.

3   Let those who say 'Aha, aha!' *
     turn back because of their shame.

4   But let all who seek you rejoice and be glad in you; *
     let those who love your salvation say always, 'The Lord is great!'

5   As for me, I am poor and needy; *
     come to me quickly, O God.

6   You are my help and my deliverer; *
     O Lord, do not delay.

PSALM 71

1   In you, O Lord, do I seek refuge; *
     let me never be put to shame.

2   In your righteousness, deliver me and set me free; *
     incline your ear to me and save me.

3   Be for me a stronghold to which I may ever resort; *
     send out to save me, for you are my rock and my fortress.

4   Deliver me, my God, from the hand of the wicked, *
     from the grasp of the evildoer and the oppressor.

5   For you are my hope, O Lord God, *
     my confidence, even from my youth.

6   I was held by you at my birth,
       when you severed me from my mother's womb; *
     my praise shall be always of you.

7   I have become a sign unto many; *
    for you are my refuge and my strength.

8   Let my mouth be full of your praise *
    and your glory all the day long.

9   Do not cast me away in the time of old age; *
    forsake me not when my strength fails.

10 For my enemies are talking against me, *
    and those who lie in wait for my life take counsel together.

11 They say, 'God has forsaken him;
        pursue him and take him; *
    because there is none to deliver him.'

12 O God, be not far from me; *
    come quickly to help me, O my God.

13 Let those who are against me
        be put to shame and disgrace; *
    let those who seek to do me evil
        be covered with scorn and reproach.

14 But as for me I will hope continually, *
    and will praise you more and more.

15 My mouth shall tell of your righteousness
        and salvation all the day long; *
    for I know no end of the telling.

16 I will begin with the mighty works of the Lord God; *
    I will recall your righteousness, yours alone.

17 O God, you have taught me since I was young, *
    and to this day I tell of your wonderful works.

18 Forsake me not, O God,
        when I am old and grey-headed, *
    till I make known your deeds to the next generation
        and your power to all that are to come.

19 Your righteousness, O God, reaches to the heavens; *
    in the great things you have done, who is like you, O God?

20 O what troubles and adversities you have shown me, *
     and yet you will turn and refresh me
        and bring me from the deep of the earth again.

21 Restore once more my honour; *
     O turn and comfort me.

22 Therefore will I praise you upon the lyre
        for your faithfulness, O my God; *
     I will sing to you with the harp, O Holy One of Israel.

23 My lips will sing out as I play to you, *
     and so will my soul, which you have redeemed.

24 My tongue also will tell of your righteousness all the day long, *
     for they shall be shamed and disgraced who sought to do me evil.

PSALM 72

1 Give the king your judgement, O God, *
    and your righteousness to the son of a king.

2 Then shall he judge your people righteously *
    and your poor with justice.

3 May the mountains bring prosperity, *
    and the little hills righteousness for the people.

4 May he defend the poor among the people; *
    deliver the children of the needy and crush the oppressor.

5 May he live as long as the sun and moon endure, *
    from one generation to another.

6 May he come down like rain upon the mown grass, *
    like the showers that water the earth.

7 In his time shall righteousness flourish; *
    and abundance of peace
        till the moon shall be no more.

8   May his dominion extend from sea to sea, *
    and from the River to the ends of the earth.

9   May his foes kneel before him; *
    and his enemies lick the dust.

10 The kings of Tarshish and of the isles shall pay tribute, *
    the kings of Arabia and Saba shall bring gifts.

11 All kings shall fall down before him, *
    all nations shall do him service.

12 For he shall deliver the poor that cry out, *
    the needy and those who have no helper.

13 He shall have pity on the weak and poor; *
    he shall preserve the lives of the needy.

14 He shall redeem their lives from oppression and violence, *
    and dear shall their blood be in his sight.

15 Long may he live;
        unto him may be given gold from Arabia; *
    may prayer be made for him continually,
        and may they bless him all the day long.

16 May there be abundance of grain on the earth,
        standing high on the hilltops; *
    may its fruit flourish like Lebanon,
        and its grain grow like the grass of the field.

17 May his name remain for ever
        and be established as long as the sun endures; *
    may all nations be blessed in him
        and call him blessèd.

18 Blessèd be the Lord, the God of Israel, *
    who alone does wonderful things!

19 And blessèd be his glorious name for ever! *
    May all the earth be filled with his glory.
        Amen. Amen.

PSALM 73

1   Truly, God is loving to Israel, *
      to those who are pure in heart.

2   Nevertheless, my feet were almost gone; *
      my steps had well-nigh slipped.

3   For I was envious of the proud; *
      I saw the wicked in such prosperity;

4   For they suffer no pains, *
      and their bodies are sleek and sound;

5   They come to no misfortune like other folk; *
      nor are they plagued as others are;

6   Therefore pride is their necklace *
      and violence wraps them like a cloak.

7   Their iniquity comes from within, *
      the conceits of their hearts overflow.

8   They scoff, and speak only of evil; *
      they talk of oppression from on high.

9   They stretch their mouth to the heavens, *
      and their tongue licks round the earth.

10   And so the people turn to them *
      and find in them no fault.

11   They say, 'How should God know? *
      Is there knowledge in the Most High?'

12   Behold, these are the wicked; *
      ever at ease, they increase their wealth.

13   Is it in vain that I cleansed my heart *
      and washed my hands in innocence?

14   All day long have I been stricken, *
      and chastened every morning.

15 If I had said, 'I will speak as they do,' *
   I should have betrayed the generation of your children.

16 Then thought I to understand this, *
   but it was too hard for me;

17 Until I entered the sanctuary of God *
   and understood the end of the wicked:

18 How you set them in slippery places; *
   you cast them down to destruction.

19 O how suddenly do they come to destruction, *
   perish and come to a fearful end!

20 Even as a dream when one awakes, *
   so, Lord, when you arise will you dispel their image.

21 When my heart became embittered, *
   and I was pierced to the quick,

22 I was but foolish and ignorant; *
   I was like a brute beast in your presence.

23 Yet I am always with you; *
   you hold me by my right hand.

24 You will guide me with your counsel, *
   and afterwards receive me with glory.

25 Whom have I in heaven but you? *
   And there is nothing upon earth that I desire
      in comparison with you.

26 Though my flesh and my heart fail me, *
   God is the strength of my heart and my portion for ever.

27 Truly, those who forsake you will perish; *
   you will put to silence the faithless who betray you.

28 But it is good for me to draw near to God; *
   in the Lord God have I made my refuge
      that I may tell of all your works.

PSALM 74

1   O God, why have you utterly disowned us? *
       Why does your anger burn
          against the sheep of your pasture?

2   Remember your congregation that you purchased of old, *
       the tribe you redeemed for your own possession,
          and Mount Zion where you dwelt.

3   Hasten your steps towards the endless ruins; *
       where the enemy has laid waste all your sanctuary.

4   Your adversaries roared in the place of your worship; *
       they set up their banners as tokens of victory.

5   They were like men brandishing axes *
       on high in a thicket of trees;

6   So then all her carved work altogether *
       they smashed down with hatchet and hammer.

7   They set fire to your holy place; *
       they defiled the dwelling-place of your name
          and razed it to the ground.

8   They said in their heart, 'Let us make havoc of them altogether'; *
       and they burned down all the sanctuaries of God in the land.

9   There are no signs to see, not one prophet left, *
       not one among us who knows how long.

10   How long, O God, will the adversary scoff? *
       Shall the enemy blaspheme your name for ever?

11   Why have you withheld your hand? *
       and hidden your right hand in your bosom?

12   Yet God is my king from of old, *
       who did deeds of salvation in the midst of the earth,

13   It was you that divided the sea by your might *
       and shattered the heads of the dragons on the waters;

14   You alone crushed the heads of Leviathan *
          and gave him to the beasts of the desert for food.

15   It was you that cleft the rock for fountain and flood; *
          you that dried up ever-flowing rivers.

16   From you came day, from you the night; *
          you alone established the moon and the sun.

17   It was you that established the bounds of the earth; *
          you fashioned both summer and winter.

18   Remember now, Lord, how the enemy scoffed, *
          how a foolish people despised your name.

19   Do not give to wild beasts the soul of your turtle-dove; *
          forget not the lives of your poor for ever.

20   Look upon your covenant,
          for the dark places of the earth are filled; *
          filled are the fields of violence.

21   Let not the oppressed turn away ashamed; *
          but let the poor and needy praise your name.

22   Arise, O God, maintain your own cause; *
          remember how fools revile you all the day long.

23   Forget not the clamour of your adversaries, *
          the tumult of your enemies that ascends continually.

PSALM 75

1   We give you thanks, O God, we give you thanks, *
          for your name is near, as your wonderful deeds declare.

2   'I will seize the appointed time; *
          I, the Lord, will judge with equity.

3   Though the earth reels and all that dwell on her, *
          I will make her pillars fast.

4   'To the boasters I say, "Boast no longer", *
    and to the wicked, "Do not lift up your horn.

5   '"Do not lift up your horn on high, *
    nor speak with an insolent neck"'.

6   For neither from the east nor from the west, *
    nor yet from the wilderness comes exaltation.

7   But God alone is the judge; *
    he puts down one and raises up another.

8   For in the hand of the Lord there is a cup *
    full of foaming wine well mixed.

9   He pours it out for all the wicked of the earth; *
    they shall drink it, and drain the dregs.

10 But I will rejoice for ever; *
    and make music to the God of Jacob.

11 All the horns of the wicked will I break; *
    but the horns of the righteous shall be exalted.

PSALM 76

1   God has revealed himself in Judah; *
    great is his name in Israel.

2   At Salem is his tabernacle, *
    and his dwelling-place in Zion.

3   There broke he the flashing arrows of the bow, *
    the shield, the sword and the line of battle.

4   In the light of splendour you appeared: *
    glorious from the mountains of prey!

5   The boastful were plundered; they have slept their sleep; *
    none of the warriors can lift their hand.

6   At your rebuke, O God of Jacob, *
    both horse and chariot fell stunned.

7   In dread majesty you appeared! *
    Who can stand before your face when you are angry?

8   You caused your judgement to be heard from heaven; *
    the earth trembled and was still;

9   When God arose to judgement *
    and to save all the meek upon earth.

10 The wrath of the peoples shall turn to your praise, *
    and the remnant of wrath you will restrain.

11 Make a vow to the Lord your God and keep it; *
    let all that are round about him bring gifts
        to him that is worthy to be feared.

12 He breaks down the spirit of princes, *
    and strikes terror in the kings of the earth.

PSALM 77

1   I cry to God with my voice; *
    to God I cry with my voice that he may hear me.

2   In the day of my trouble I have sought the Lord; *
    by night my hand is stretched out and does not tire;
        my soul refuses comfort.

3   I think upon God and I groan; *
    I ponder, and my spirit faints.

4   You will not let my eyelids close; *
    I am so troubled that I cannot speak.

5   I consider the days of old; *
    I remember the years long past;

6   I commune with my heart in the night; *
    I ponder and search my spirit.

7   Will the Lord cast me off for ever? *
    Will he no more show us his favour?

8   Has his loving mercy clean gone for ever? *
    Has his promise come to an end for evermore?

9   Has God forgotten to be gracious? *
    Has he shut up his compassion in displeasure?

10 And I said, 'My grief is this: *
    that the right hand of the Most High has changed.'

11 I will remember the works of the Lord, *
    and call to mind your wonders of old time.

12 I will meditate on all your works *
    and sing of your mighty deeds.

13 Your way, O God, is holy; *
    who is so great a god as our God?

14 You are the God who worked wonders *
    and have declared your power among the peoples.

15 With a mighty arm you redeemed your people, *
    the children of Jacob and Joseph.

16 The waters saw you, O God;
        the waters saw you and were afraid; *
    the depths also were troubled.

17 The clouds poured out water; the skies thundered; *
    your arrows flashed on every side;

18 The voice of your thunder was in the whirlwind;
        your lightnings lit up the ground; *
    the earth trembled and shook.

19 Your way was in the sea, and your paths in the great waters, *
    but your footsteps were not known.

20 You led your people like sheep *
    by the hand of Moses and Aaron.

PSALM 78

1 Hear my teaching, O my people; *
  incline your ears to the words of my mouth.

2 I will open my mouth in a parable; *
  I will pour forth mysteries from of old

3 Such as we have heard and known, *
  which our forebears have told us.

4 We will not hide from their children,
   but will recount to generations to come: *
  the praises of the Lord and his power,
   and the wonderful works he has done.

5 He laid a solemn charge on Jacob
   and made it a law in Israel, *
  which he commanded them to teach their children;

6 That the generations to come might know,
   and the children yet unborn; *
  that they in turn might tell it to their children;

7 So that they might put their trust in God, *
  and not forget the deeds of God,
   but keep his commandments;

8 And not be like their forebears,
   a stubborn and rebellious generation, *
  a generation whose heart was not steadfast,
   and whose spirit was not faithful to God.

9 The people of Ephraim, armed with the bow, *
  turned back in the day of battle;

10 They did not keep the covenant of God, *
  and refused to walk in his law;

11 They forgot what he had done, *
  and the wonders he had shown them.

12 For he did marvellous things in the sight of their forebears, *
in the land of Egypt, in the field of Zoan.

13 He divided the sea and let them pass through; *
he made the waters stand still in a heap.

14 He led them with a cloud by day, *
and all the night through with a blaze of fire.

15 He split the hard rocks in the wilderness *
and gave them drink as from the great deep.

16 He brought streams out of the rock *
and made water gush out like rivers.

17 Yet for all this they sinned more against him, *
and defied the Most High in the wilderness.

18 They tested God in their hearts, *
and demanded food for their craving.

19 They spoke against God and said, *
'Can God prepare a table in the wilderness?

20 'He struck the rock indeed, so that the waters gushed out,
and the streams overflowed; *
but can he give bread or provide meat for his people?'

21 When the Lord heard this, he was full of wrath; *
a fire was kindled against Jacob,
and his anger went out against Israel;

22 For they had no faith in God, *
and put no trust in his saving help.

23 So he commanded the clouds above *
and opened the doors of heaven.

24 He rained down upon them manna to eat *
and gave them the grain of heaven.

25 So mortals ate the bread of angels; *
he sent them food in plenty.

26 He caused the east wind to blow in the heavens *
and led out the south wind by his might.

27 He rained flesh upon them as thick as dust *
and winged fowl like the sand of the sea.

28 He let it fall in the midst of their camp *
and round about their tents.

29 So they ate and were well filled, *
for he gave them what they desired.

30 But they did not stop their craving; *
their food was still in their mouths

31 When the anger of God rose against them *
and slew their strongest men,
and felled the choicest of Israel.

32 But for all this, they sinned yet more *
and put no faith in his wonderful works.

33 So he brought their days to an end like a breath *
and their years in sudden terror.

34 Whenever he slew them, they would seek him, *
they would repent and earnestly search for God.

35 They remembered that God was their rock, *
and the Most High God their redeemer.

36 Yet they did but flatter him with their mouth *
and dissembled with their tongue.

37 Their heart was not steadfast towards him, *
neither were they faithful to his covenant.

38 But he was so merciful that he forgave their misdeeds
and did not destroy them; *
many a time he turned back his wrath
and did not suffer his whole displeasure to be roused.

39   For he remembered that they were but flesh, *
a wind that passes by and does not return.

40   How often they rebelled against him in the wilderness *
and grieved him in the desert!

41   Again and again they tempted God *
and provoked the Holy One of Israel.

42   They did not remember his power *
in the day when he redeemed them from the enemy;

43   How he had wrought his signs in Egypt *
and his wonders in the field of Zoan.

44   He turned their rivers into blood, *
so that they could not drink of their streams.

45   He sent swarms of flies among them, which devoured them, *
and frogs which brought them ruin.

46   He gave their produce to the caterpillar, *
the fruit of their toil to the locust.

47   He destroyed their vines with hailstones *
and their mulberry trees with the frost.

48   He delivered their cattle to hailstones *
and their flocks to hot thunderbolts.

49   He set loose on them his blazing anger: *
fury, displeasure and trouble,
    a troop of destroying angels.

50   He made a way for his anger,
    and spared not their souls from death; *
but gave their life over to the pestilence.

51   He smote the first-born of Egypt, *
the first-fruits of their strength in the land of Ham.

52   But he led out his people like sheep *
and guided them in the wilderness like a flock.

53 He led them to safety and they were not afraid; *
    but the sea overwhelmed their enemies.

54 He brought them to his holy place, *
    the mountain his right hand took in possession.

55 He drove out the nations before them
        and shared out to them their inheritance; *
    he settled the tribes of Israel in their tents.

56 Yet still they tested God Most High
        and rebelled against him, *
    and would not keep his commandments.

57 They turned back and fell away like their forebears; *
    starting aside like a twisted bow.

58 They grieved him with their hill-altars *
    and provoked him to displeasure with their idols.

59 God heard and was greatly angered; *
    and utterly rejected Israel.

60 He forsook the tabernacle at Shiloh, *
    the tent of his presence on earth.

61 He gave the ark of his glory into captivity, *
    his splendour into the adversary's hand.

62 He delivered his people to the sword *
    and raged against his inheritance.

63 The fire consumed their young men; *
    and their maidens were not given in marriage.

64 Their priests fell by the sword, *
    and their widows made no lamentation.

65 Then the Lord woke as out of sleep, *
    like a warrior refreshed with wine.

66 He struck his enemies in the rear *
    and put them to perpetual shame.

67 He rejected the tent of Joseph *
and chose not the tribe of Ephraim;

68 But he chose the tribe of Judah *
and the hill of Zion, which he loved.

69 And there he built his sanctuary like the heights of heaven, *
like the earth which he founded for ever.

70 He chose David also, his servant, *
and took him away from the sheepfolds.

71 From following the ewes with their lambs he took him, *
that he might shepherd Jacob his people
and Israel his inheritance.

72 So he shepherded them with a devoted heart *
and with skilful hands he guided them.

PSALM 79

1 O God, the heathen have come into your heritage; *
your holy temple have they defiled,
and made Jerusalem a heap of stones.

2 The dead bodies of your servants have they given
to be food for the birds of the air, *
and the flesh of your faithful to the beasts of the field.

3 Their blood have they shed like water
on every side of Jerusalem, *
and there was no one to bury them.

4 We have become the taunt of our neighbours, *
the scorn and derision of those that are round about us.

5 Lord, how long will you be angry, for ever? *
how long will your jealous fury blaze like fire?

6 Pour out your wrath upon the nations that have not known you *
and upon the kingdoms that have not called upon your name.

7 For they have devoured Jacob *
and laid waste his dwelling-place.

8   Remember not against us our former sins; *
    let your compassion make haste to meet us,
        for we are brought very low.

9   Help us, O God of our salvation, for the glory of your name; *
    O deliver us, and wipe away our sins for your name's sake.

10 Why should the heathen say, *
    'Where is now their God?'

11 Let the avenging of your servants' blood that is shed *
    be known among the nations in our sight.

12 Let the sorrowful sighing of the prisoners come before you, *
    and by your mighty arm,
        preserve those who are condemned to die.

13 May the taunts with which our neighbours taunted you, O Lord, *
    return sevenfold into their bosom.

14 But we that are your people and the sheep of your pasture *
    will give you thanks for ever,
        and tell of your praise from generation to generation.

PSALM 80

1   Hear, O Shepherd of Israel, *
    you that led Joseph like a flock; *

2   Shine forth, you that are enthroned upon the cherubim *
    before Ephraim, Benjamin and Manasseh.

3   Stir up your mighty strength *
    and come to our salvation.

4   *Turn us again, O God; *
    show the light of your countenance, and we shall be saved.*

5   O Lord God of hosts, *
    how long will you be angry at your people's prayer?

6   You feed them with the bread of tears; *
    you give them abundance of tears to drink.

7 You have made us the derision of our neighbours, *
  and our enemies laugh us to scorn.

8 *Turn us again, O God of hosts; ***
  show the light of your countenance, and we shall be saved.

9 You brought a vine out of Egypt; *
  you drove out the nations and planted it.

10 You made room around it; *
  and when it had taken root, it filled the land.

11 The hills were covered with its shadow *
  and the cedars of God by its boughs.

12 She stretched out her branches to the Sea *
  and her tendrils to the River.

13 Why then have you broken down her wall, *
  so that all who pass by pluck off her grapes?

14 The wild boar out of the wood roots it up, *
  and all the beasts of the field devour it.

15 Turn again, O God of hosts, *
  look down from heaven and behold;

16 Cherish this vine which your right hand has planted; *
  and the branch that you made so strong for yourself.

17 It is cut away and burnt in the fire; *
  they perish at the rebuke of your countenance.

18 Let your hand be upon the man at your right hand, *
  the son of man you made so strong for yourself.

19 And so will we not go back from you; *
  O give us life, and we shall declare your name.

20 *Turn us again, O Lord God of hosts; ***
  show the light of your countenance, and we shall be saved.

PSALM 81

1   O sing merrily to God our strength *
      make cheerful praise to the God of Jacob.

2   Take up the song and sound the timbrel, *
      the merry harp and the lyre.

3   Blow the trumpet at the new moon, *
      as at the full moon, upon our solemn feast-day.

4   For this is a statute for Israel, *
      a law of the God of Jacob;

5   The charge he laid on the people of Joseph, *
      when they came out of the land of Egypt.

6   I heard a voice I did not know, that said: *
      'I eased their shoulder from the burden;
        their hands were set free from bearing the loads.'

7   You called upon me in trouble and I delivered you; *
      I answered you from the secret place of thunder
        and proved you at the waters of Meribah.

8   Hear, O my people, and I will admonish you: *
      O Israel, if you would but listen to me!

9   There shall no strange god be among you; *
      you shall not worship a foreign god.

10   I am the Lord your God,
        who brought you out of the land of Egypt, *
      'Open wide your mouth and I shall fill it.'

11   But my people would not hear my voice, *
      and Israel would not obey me.

12   So I sent them away in the stubbornness of their hearts, *
      and let them walk after their own counsels.

13   O that my people would listen to me, *
      that Israel would walk in my ways!

14   Then should I soon put down their enemies *
     and turn my hand against their adversaries.

15   Those who hate the Lord would be humbled before him, *
     and their punishment would last for ever.

16   But Israel would I feed with the finest wheat *
     and with honey from the rock would I satisfy them.

PSALM 82

1   God has taken his stand in the council of heaven; *
     in the midst of the gods he gives judgement:

2   'How long will you judge unjustly, *
     and show such favour to the wicked?

3   'You were to judge the weak and the orphan; *
     defend the right of the humble and needy;

4   'Rescue the weak and the poor; *
     deliver them from the hand of the wicked.

5   'They have no knowledge or wisdom;
         they walk on still in darkness: *
     all the foundations of the earth are shaken.

6   'Therefore I say that though you are gods, *
     and all of you children of the Most High,

7   'Nevertheless, you shall die like mortals, *
     and fall like one of their princes.'

8   Arise, O God; judge the earth, *
     for it is you that shall take all nations for your own possession.

PSALM 83

1   Hold not your peace, O God, do not keep silent; *
     be not unmoved, O God;

2   For your enemies are in tumult, *
    and those who hate you lift up their heads.

3   They take secret counsel against your people *
    and plot against those whom you treasure.

4   They say, 'Come, let us destroy them as a nation *
    that the name of Israel be remembered no more.'

5   They have conspired together with one mind; *
    they are in league against you:

6   The tents of Edom and the Ishmaelites, *
    Moab and the Hagarenes,

7   Gebal and Ammon and Amalek, *
    the Philistines and those who dwell in Tyre.

8   Ashur also has joined them, *
    and has become the arm for the children of Lot.

9   Do to them as you did to Midian, *
    to Sisera and to Jabin at the river of Kishon:

10   Who perished at Endor; *
    and became as dung for the earth.

11   Make their commanders like Oreb and Zeëb, *
    and all their princes like Zebah and Zalmunna,

12   Who said, 'Let us take for ourselves *
    the pastures of God as our possession.'

13   O my God, make them like thistledown, *
    like chaff before the wind;

14   Like fire that burns through a forest, *
    like the flame that sets mountains ablaze.

15   So drive them with your tempest *
    and dismay them with your storm;

16   Cover their faces with shame, O Lord, *
    that they may seek your name.

17 Let them be disgraced and dismayed for ever; *
    let them be put to confusion and perish.

18 And they shall know that you, whose name is the Lord, *
    are alone the Most High over all the earth.

PSALM 84

1   How lovely is your dwelling-place, O Lord of hosts! *
    My soul has a desire and longing to enter the courts of the Lord;
        my heart and my flesh rejoice in the living God.

2   The sparrow has found her a house
        and the swallow a nest where she may lay her young; *
    at your altars, O Lord of hosts, my King and my God.

3   Blessed are they who dwell in your house! *
    They will always be praising you.

4   Blessed are those whose strength is in you, *
    in whose heart are the highways to Zion;

5   Who going through the barren valley find there a spring; *
    and the early rains will clothe it with blessing.

6   They will go from strength to strength, *
    and appear before God in Zion.

7   O Lord God of hosts, hear my prayer; *
    hearken, O God of Jacob.

8   Behold our defender, O God; *
    and look upon the face of your anointed.

9   For one day in your courts *
    is better than a thousand.

10 I would rather be a doorkeeper in the house of my God *
    than dwell in the tents of ungodliness.

11 For the Lord God is both sun and shield;
        he will give grace and glory; *
    no good thing shall he withhold from those who walk with
        integrity.

12 O Lord God of hosts, *
    blessed are they who put their trust in you!

PSALM 85

1   Lord, you were gracious to your land, *
    you restored the fortunes of Jacob.

2   You forgave the offence of your people *
    and covered all their sins.

3   You laid aside all your fury *
    and turned from your wrathful indignation.

4   Restore us again, O God our Saviour; *
    and let your anger cease from us.

5   Will you be displeased with us for ever? *
    Will you stretch out your wrath from one generation to another?

6   Will you not give us life again, *
    that your people may rejoice in you?

7   Show us your mercy, O Lord, *
    and grant us your salvation.

8   I will listen to what the Lord God will say, *
    for he shall speak peace to his people and to the faithful,
        that they turn not again to folly.

9   Truly, his salvation is near to those who fear him, *
    that his glory may dwell in our land.

10 Mercy and truth are met together; *
    righteousness and peace have kissed each other.

11 Truth shall spring up from the earth, *
    and righteousness look down from heaven.

12   The Lord will indeed give his blessing, *
and our land will yield its increase.

13   Righteousness shall go before him, *
and prepare the way for his steps.

PSALM 86

1   Incline your ear, O Lord, and answer me, *
for I am poor and in misery.

2   Preserve my soul, for I am faithful; *
O save your servant, for I put my trust in you.

3   Be merciful to me, O Lord, for you are my God; *
I call upon you all the day long.

4   Gladden the soul of your servant, *
for to you, O Lord, I lift up my soul.

5   For you, O Lord, are gracious and merciful, *
abounding in steadfast love to all who call upon you.

6   Give ear, O Lord, to my prayer, *
and listen to the voice of my supplication.

7   In the day of my distress I will call upon you, *
for you will answer me.

8   Among the gods there is none like you, O Lord, *
nor any works like yours.

9   All nations you have made shall come and worship you, O Lord, *
and shall glorify your name.

10   For you are great and do wonderful things; *
you alone are God.

11   Teach me your way, O Lord, and I will walk in your truth; *
O knit my heart to you, that I may fear your name.

12   I will thank you, O Lord my God, with all my heart, *
      and glorify your name for evermore;

13   For great is your steadfast love towards me; *
      for you have delivered my soul from the depths of hell.

14   O God, the proud rise up against me,
        and a ruthless horde seek after my life; *
      they have not set you before their eyes.

15   But you, O Lord, are gracious and full of compassion, *
      slow to anger and full of kindness and truth.

16   O turn to me and have mercy upon me; *
      give your strength to your servant
        and save the child of your handmaid.

17   Show me a token of your favour,
        that those who hate me may see it and be ashamed; *
      because you, O Lord, have helped me and comforted me.

PSALM 87

1   The Lord loves his foundation on the holy mountains, *
      the gates of Zion more than all the dwellings of Jacob.

2   Glorious things are spoken of you, *
      Zion, city of our God.

3   I record Egypt and Babylon as those who know me; *
      behold Philistia, Tyre and Ethiopia:
        in Zion were they born.

4   And of Zion it shall be said, 'Each one was born in her, *
      and the Most High himself has established her.'

5   The Lord will record as he writes up the peoples, *
      'This one also was born there.'

6   And as they dance they shall sing, *
      'All my fresh springs are in you.'

PSALM 88

1   O Lord, God of my salvation, *
     I have cried day and night before you.

2   Let my prayer come into your presence; *
     incline your ear to my cry.

3   For my soul is full of troubles; *
     my life draws near to the land of death.

4   I am counted as one gone down to the Pit; *
     I am like one that has no strength;

5   My couch is among the dead, *
     like the slain who lie in the grave,

6   Whom you remember no more, *
     for they are cut off from your hand.

7   You have laid me in the lowest pit, *
     in a place of darkness in the abyss.

8   Your anger lies heavy upon me, *
     and you have afflicted me with all your waves.

9   You have put my friends far from me *
     and made me to be abhorred by them.

10   I am so fast in prison that I cannot get free; *
     my eyes fail from all my trouble.

11   Lord, I have called daily upon you; *
     I have stretched out my hands to you.

12   Do you work wonders for the dead? *
     will the shades stand up and praise you?

13   Shall your loving-kindness be declared in the grave? *
     your faithfulness in the land of destruction?

14   Shall your wonders be known in the dark? *
     or your righteous deeds in the land where all is forgotten?

15 But as for me, O Lord, I will cry to you; *
   early in the morning my prayer shall come before you.

16 Lord, why have you rejected my soul? *
   Why have you hidden your face from me?

17 I am wretched and at the point of death from my youth; *
   I suffer your terrors and I pass away.

18 Your wrath sweeps over me; *
   your horrors are come to destroy me;

19 All day long they come about me like water; *
   they close me in on every side.

20 Lover and friend have you put far from me, *
   and hid my companions out of my sight.

PSALM 89

1 My song shall be always of the loving-kindness of the Lord: *
   with my mouth will I proclaim your faithfulness throughout all
      generations.

2 I will declare that your love is established for ever; *
   you have set your faithfulness as firm as the heavens.

3 For you said: 'I have made a covenant with my chosen one; *
   I have sworn an oath to David my servant:

4 '"Your seed will I establish for ever, *
   and build up your throne for all generations."'

5 The heavens bear witness to your wonders, O Lord, *
   and to your faithfulness in the assembly of the holy ones;

6 For who among the clouds can be compared to the Lord? *
   Who is like the Lord among the host of heaven?

7 A God feared in the council of the holy ones, *
   great and terrible above all those round about him.

8   O Lord God of hosts, who is mighty like you? *
     Your faithfulness is all around you.

9   You rule the raging of the sea *
     you still its waves when they arise.

10   You crushed Rahab with a deadly wound; *
     and scattered your enemies with your mighty arm.

11   Yours are the heavens; the earth also is yours; *
     you established the world and all that fills it.

12   You created the mountains of the north and the south; *
     Tabor and Hermon rejoice in your name.

13   You have a mighty arm; *
     strong is your hand and high is your right hand.

14   Righteousness and justice are the foundation of your throne; *
     steadfast love and faithfulness go before your face.

15   Happy are the people who know the praises of your glory; *
     they walk, O Lord, in the light of your countenance.

16   In your name they rejoice all the day long; *
     and are exalted in your righteousness.

17   For you are the glory of their strength; *
     and in your favour you lift up our heads.

18   Truly the Lord is our shield, *
     the Holy One of Israel is our king.

19   You spoke once in a vision and said to your faithful people: *
     'I have set a youth above the mighty;
         I have raised a young man over the people.

20   'I have found David my servant; *
     with my holy oil have I anointed him.

21   'My hand shall hold him fast *
     and my arm shall strengthen him.

22 'No enemy shall deceive him; *
    nor any wicked person afflict him.

23 'I will strike down his foes before his face, *
    and beat down those that hate him.

24 'My truth also and my steadfast love shall be with him *
    and in my name shall his horn be exalted.

25 'I will set his dominion upon the sea, *
    and his right hand upon the rivers.

26 'He shall call to me, "You are my Father, *
    my God, and the rock of my salvation."

27 'And I will make him my first-born: *
    the most high above the kings of the earth.

28 'The love I have pledged to him will I keep for ever *
    and my covenant will stand fast with him.

29 'His seed also will I make to endure for ever *
    and his throne as the days of heaven.

30 'But if his children forsake my law, *
    and cease to walk in my judgements,

31 'If they break my statutes *
    and do not keep my commandments,

32 'I will punish their offences with a rod *
    and their sin with scourges.

33 'But I will not take from him my steadfast love *
    nor suffer my truth to fail.

34 'My covenant will I not break *
    nor alter what has gone out of my lips.

35 'Once for all have I sworn by my holiness *
    that I will not prove false to David.

36 'His seed shall endure for ever *
    and his throne as the sun before me;

37 'It shall stand fast for ever as the moon, *
    the enduring witness in the heavens.'

38 But you have cast off and rejected your anointed; *
    you have shown fierce anger against him.

39 You have broken the covenant with your servant, *
    and have cast his crown to the ground.

40 You have broken down all his walls, *
    and laid his strongholds in ruins.

41 All who pass by despoil him *
    and he has become the scorn of his neighbours.

42 You have exalted the right hand of his foes *
    and made all his enemies rejoice.

43 You have turned back the edge of his sword *
    and have not upheld him in battle.

44 You have made an end of his radiance *
    and cast his throne to the ground.

45 You have cut short the days of his youth *
    and have covered him with shame.

46 How long will you hide yourself, O Lord, so utterly? *
    How long shall your anger burn like fire?

47 Remember how short my time is; *
    how frail you have made all the children of earth.

48 Which of the living shall not see death, *
    and shall deliver their soul from the land of darkness?

49 Where are your promises of old *
    which you swore to David in your faithfulness?

50 Remember, O Lord, how your servant is scorned; *
    how I bear in my bosom the taunts of many peoples,

51 While your enemies mock, O Lord, *
    while they mock the footsteps of your Anointed.

52 Blessed be the Lord for evermore. *
    Amen and Amen.

PSALM 90

1   Lord, you have been our refuge *
    from one generation to another.

2   Before the mountains were born,
        or the earth and the world brought forth, *
    from everlasting to everlasting, you are God.

3   You turn us back to dust and say: *
    'Turn back, O children of earth.'

4   For a thousand years in your sight are but as yesterday, *
    for they pass like a watch in the night.

5   You sweep us away like a dream; *
    we fade away suddenly like the grass.

6   In the morning it is green and flourishes; *
    in the evening it is dried up and withered.

7   For we consume away in your displeasure; *
    we are afraid at your wrathful indignation.

8   You have set our misdeeds before you, *
    and our secret sins in the light of your countenance.

9   When you are angry, all our days are gone; *
    our years come to an end like a sigh.

10 The days of our life are three score years and ten,
        or if our strength endures, even four score; *
    yet the sum of them is but labour and sorrow,
        for they soon pass away and we are gone.

11 Who regards the power of your wrath? *
    Who rightly fears your indignation?

12   So teach us to number our days *
      that we may apply our hearts to wisdom.

13   Turn again, O Lord; how long will you delay? *
      Be gracious to your servants.

14   Satisfy us with your loving-kindness in the morning; *
      that we may rejoice and be glad in all our days.

15   Make us glad for as many days as you have afflicted us *
      and for the years in which we have seen adversity.

16   Show your servants your works *
      and let your glory be over their children.

17   May the gracious favour of the Lord our God be upon us; *
      prosper the work of our hands; O prosper our handiwork!

PSALM 91

1   Whoever dwells in the shelter of the Most High, *
      and abides under the shadow of the Almighty,

2   Shall say to the Lord, 'My refuge and my stronghold, *
      my God, in whom I put my trust.'

3   For he shall deliver you from the snare of the fowler *
      and from the deadly curse.

4   He shall cover you with his wings,
       and you shall be safe under his feathers; *
      his faithfulness shall be your shield and buckler.

5   You shall not be afraid of any terror by night, *
      nor of the arrow that flies by day;

6   Of the pestilence that stalks in darkness, *
      nor of the sickness that destroys at noonday.

7   Though a thousand fall at your side
       and ten thousand at your right hand, *
      yet it shall not come near you.

8   Your eyes have only to behold *
     to see the reward of the wicked.

9   Because you have made the Lord your refuge, *
     and the Most High your stronghold,

10   There shall no evil happen to you, *
     neither shall any plague come near your tent.

11   For he shall give his angels charge over you, *
     to keep you in all your ways.

12   They shall bear you in their hands, *
     lest you dash your foot against a stone.

13   You shall tread upon the dragon and adder; *
     the lion and the serpent you shall trample under your feet.

14   Because you have set your love upon me,
        therefore will I deliver you; *
     I will lift you up, because you know my name.

15   You will call upon me and I will answer you; *
     I am with you in trouble,
        I will deliver you and bring you to honour.

16   With long life will I satisfy you; *
     and show you my salvation.

PSALM 92

1   It is a good thing to give thanks to the Lord, *
     and to sing praises to your name, O Most High;

2   To tell of your love early in the morning *
     and of your faithfulness in the night-time;

3   Upon the ten-stringed instrument, upon the lyre, *
     and to the melody of the harp.

4   For you, Lord, have made me glad by your acts; *
     and I sing aloud at the works of your hands.

5   O Lord, how glorious are your works! *
    Your thoughts are very deep.

6   The senseless does not know, *
    nor do fools understand,

7   That though the wicked sprout like grass *
    and all the workers of iniquity flourish,

8   It is only to be destroyed for ever; *
    but you, O Lord, shall be exalted for evermore.

9   For lo, your enemies, O Lord,
      lo, your enemies shall perish, *
    and all the workers of iniquity shall be scattered.

10   But my horn you have exalted
      like the horns of wild oxen; *
    I am anointed with fresh oil.

11   My eyes shall see the flight of my foes, *
    and my ears shall hear the confusion of all who rise up against me.

12   The righteous shall flourish like a palm tree, *
    and shall spread abroad like a cedar of Lebanon.

13   Such as are planted in the house of the Lord *
    shall flourish in the courts of our God.

14   They shall still bear fruit in old age; *
    they shall be vigorous and full of life;

15   That they may show that the Lord is true, *
    my rock, in whom there is no unrighteousness.

PSALM 93

1   The Lord is king and has put on glorious apparel; *
    the Lord has put on his glory
      and girded himself with strength.

2   He has made the whole world so sure *
    that it cannot be moved.

3 From of old has your throne been established; *
   you are from everlasting.

4 The floods have lifted up, O Lord,
      the floods have lifted up their voice; *
   the floods lift up their pounding waves.

5 Mightier than the thunder of many waters,
      mightier than the breakers of the sea, *
   mightier is the Lord on high.

6 Your testimonies are very sure, *
   and holiness adorns your house, O Lord, for ever.

PSALM 94

1 Lord God to whom vengeance belongs, *
   O God to whom vengeance belongs, shine out in majesty.

2 Rise up, O Judge of the earth; *
   give the arrogant their just deserts.

3 How long shall the wicked, O Lord, *
   how long shall the wicked triumph?

4 How long shall the evildoers boast *
   and pour out such cruel words?

5 Your people, O Lord, they crush *
   and afflict your heritage.

6 The widow and the stranger they murder *
   the orphans they put to death.

7 And yet they say, 'The Lord will not see; *
   neither shall the God of Jacob regard it.'

8 Consider, most stupid of people; *
   you fools, when will you understand?

9 He that planted the ear, shall he not hear? *
   He that formed the eye, shall he not see?

10 He who corrects the nations, shall he not punish? *
   He who teaches the peoples, shall he lack knowledge?

11 The Lord knows the thoughts of the heart; *
   that they are like a breath.

12 Happy are those whom you chasten, O Lord! *
   whom you teach out of your law;

13 That you may give them rest in days of adversity, *
   until a pit is dug for the wicked.

14 For the Lord will not fail his people, *
   nor will he forsake his inheritance.

15 For justice shall return to the righteous, *
   and all that are true of heart shall follow it.

16 Who will rise up for me against the wicked? *
   Who will take my part against the evildoers?

17 If the Lord had not helped me, *
   my soul would soon have been put to silence.

18 And when I said, 'My foot has slipped', *
   your loving mercy, O Lord, upheld me.

19 In the multitude of cares that troubled my heart, *
   your comforts have refreshed my soul.

20 Will you have anything to do with the throne of wickedness, *
   which fashions mischief through its law?

21 They gather together against the life of the righteous *
   and condemn the innocent to death.

22 But the Lord has become my stronghold, *
   and my God the rock of my trust.

23 He will turn against them their own wickedness
      and silence them with their own malice; *
   the Lord our God will put them to silence.

PSALM 95

1   O come, let us sing to the Lord; *
let us heartily rejoice in the rock of our salvation.

2   Let us come into his presence with thanksgiving *
and be glad in him with psalms.

3   For the Lord is a great God, *
and a great king above all gods.

4   In his hand are the depths of the earth, *
and the heights of the mountains are his also.

5   The sea is his, for he made it, *
and his hands have moulded the dry land.

6   Come, let us worship and bow down, *
and kneel before the Lord our Maker.

7   For he is our God, *
and we are the people of his pasture and the sheep of his hand.

8   O that today you would listen to his voice: *
'Harden not your hearts as at Meribah,
on that day at Massah in the wilderness,

9   'When your forebears tested me, and put me to the proof, *
though they had seen my works.

10   'Forty years long was I grieved with that generation and said, *
"This people are wayward in their hearts;
they do not know my ways."

11   'So I swore in my wrath, *
They shall not enter into my rest.'

PSALM 96

1   O sing to the Lord a new song; *
      sing to the Lord, all the earth.

2   Sing to the Lord and bless his name; *
      tell out his salvation from day to day.

3   Declare his glory among the nations *
      and his wonders among all peoples.

4   For great is the Lord and greatly to be praised; *
      he is more to be feared than all gods.

5   For all the gods of the nations are but idols; *
      it is the Lord who made the heavens.

6   Honour and majesty are before him; *
      power and splendour are in his sanctuary!

7   Ascribe to the Lord, you families of peoples; *
      ascribe to the Lord honour and strength.

8   Ascribe to the Lord the honour due to his name; *
      bring offerings and come into his courts.

9   O worship the Lord in the beauty of holiness; *
      let the whole earth tremble before him.

10   Tell it out among the nations that the Lord is king. *
      He has made the world so sure that it cannot be moved;
        he will judge the peoples with equity.

11   Let the heavens rejoice and let the earth be glad; *
      let the sea thunder and all that is in it;

12   Let the fields be joyful and all that is in them; *
      let all the trees of the wood shout for joy before the Lord.

13   For he comes, he comes to judge the earth; *
      with righteousness shall he judge the world
        and the peoples with his truth.

PSALM 97

1   The Lord is king! Let the earth rejoice; *
let the multitude of the isles be glad.

2   Clouds and darkness are round about him, *
righteousness and justice are the foundation of his throne.

3   Fire went before him *
and burnt up his enemies on every side.

4   His lightnings lit up the world; *
the earth saw it and trembled.

5   The mountains melted like wax at the presence of the Lord, *
at the presence of the Lord of the whole earth.

6   The heavens declared his righteousness, *
and all the peoples have seen his glory.

7   Confounded be all who worship carved idols
and take pride in vain nothings! *
Bow down before him, all you gods.

8   Zion heard and was glad, and the daughters of Judah rejoiced, *
because of your judgements, O Lord.

9   For you, Lord, are most high over all the earth; *
you are exalted far above all gods.

10   The Lord loves those who hate evil; *
he preserves the lives of his faithful
and delivers them from the hand of the wicked.

11   Light has sprung up for the righteous, *
and joy for the true of heart.

12   Rejoice in the Lord, you righteous, *
and give thanks to his holy name.

PSALM 98

1   Sing to the Lord a new song, *
    for he has done marvellous things.

2   His own right hand and his holy arm *
    have won for him the victory.

3   The Lord has made known his salvation; *
    his righteousness has he openly shown in the sight of the nations.

4   He has remembered his mercy and faithfulness
        towards the house of Israel, *
    and all the ends of the earth have seen the salvation of our God.

5   Sound praises to the Lord, all the earth; *
    break into singing and make music.

6   Make music to the Lord with the harp, *
    with the harp and the voice of melody.

7   With trumpets and the sound of the horn *
    sound praises before the Lord, the King.

8   Let the sea thunder and all that fills it, *
    the world and all that dwell upon it.

9   Let the rivers clap their hands, *
    and let the hills ring out together before the Lord,
        for he comes to judge the earth.

10 In righteousness shall he judge the world, *
    and the peoples with equity.

PSALM 99

1   The Lord is king! Let the peoples tremble; *
    he is enthroned above the cherubim; let the earth shake.

2   The Lord is great in Zion; *
    and high above all peoples.

3   Let them praise your name, which is great and awesome; *
    the Lord our God is holy.

4   'Mighty King, lover of justice, you have established equity; *
    you have executed justice and righteousness in Jacob.

5   *Exalt the Lord our God; **
    bow down before his footstool; for he is holy.

6   Moses and Aaron among his priests,
        and Samuel among those who call upon his name, *
    they called upon the Lord and he answered them.

7   He spoke to them out of the pillar of cloud; *
    they kept his testimonies and the law that he gave them.

8   You answered them, O Lord our God; *
    you were a God who forgave them,
        and pardoned them for their offences.

9   *Exalt the Lord our God*
        *and worship him upon his holy hill; **
    for the Lord our God is holy.

PSALM 100

1   O be joyful in the Lord, all the earth; *
    serve the Lord with gladness
        and come before his presence with a song.

2   Know that the Lord is God; *
    it is he that has made us and we are his;
        we are his people and the sheep of his pasture.

3   Enter his gates with thanksgiving,
        and his courts with praise; *
    give thanks to him and bless his name.

4   For the Lord is gracious; his love is everlasting; *
    and his faithfulness endures from generation to generation.

PSALM 101

1   I will sing of faithfulness and justice; *
    to you, O Lord, will I sing.

2   My song shall be of the perfect way – *
    O when will you come to me?

3   I will walk with purity of heart *
    within the walls of my house.

4   I will not set before my eyes *
    a counsel that is evil.

5   I abhor the deeds of unfaithfulness; *
    they shall not cling to me.

6   A crooked heart shall depart from me; *
    I will not know a wicked person.

7   One who slanders a neighbour in secret *
    I will quickly put to silence.

8   Haughty eyes and an arrogant heart – *
    I will not suffer them.

9   My eyes are upon the faithful in the land, *
    that they might dwell with me.

10 One that walks in the way that is pure *
    shall be my servant.

11 There shall not dwell in my house, *
    one that practises deceit.

12 One who utters falsehood *
    shall not continue in my sight.

13 Morning by morning will I put to silence *
    all the wicked in the land,

14 To cut off from the city of the Lord *
    all those who practise evil.

PSALM 102

1   O Lord, hear my prayer *
     and let my crying come before you.

2   Hide not your face from me *
     in the day of my distress.

3   Incline your ear to me; *
     when I call, make haste to answer me,

4   For my days are consumed in smoke, *
     and my bones burn away like a firebrand.

5   My heart is smitten down and withered like grass, *
     so that I forget to eat my bread.

6   My jaws are weary from my groaning *
     and my bones cleave fast to my skin.

7   I am become like a vulture in the wilderness, *
     like an owl that haunts the ruins.

8   I keep watch and am become *
     like a solitary sparrow on the house-top.

9   My enemies revile me all the day long, *
     and those who rage at me have sworn together against me.

10   I have eaten ashes for bread *
     and mingled my drink with weeping,

11   Because of your indignation and wrath, *
     for you have taken me up and cast me down.

12   My days fade away like a shadow, *
     and I am withered like grass.

13   But you, O Lord, shall endure for ever, *
     and your name through all generations.

14   You will arise and have pity on Zion, *
     it is time to have mercy upon her;
       surely the time has come.

15   For your servants love her very stones, *
and feel compassion for her dust.

16   Then shall the nations fear your name, O Lord, *
and all the kings of the earth your glory.

17   When the Lord shall have built up Zion, *
and shown himself in glory;

18   When he has turned to the prayer of the destitute, *
and has not despised their plea.

19   This shall be written for those that come after, *
and a people yet unborn shall praise the Lord.

20   For he has looked down from his holy height; *
from the heavens he beheld the earth;

21   That he might hear the sighings of the prisoner *
and set free those condemned to die;

22   That the name of the Lord may be proclaimed in Zion, *
and his praises in Jerusalem;

23   When the peoples are gathered together, *
and their kingdoms also, to serve the Lord.

24   He has brought down my strength in my journey; *
and has shortened my days.

25   I pray, 'O my God; do not take me in the midst of my days; *
your years endure throughout all generations.

26   'In the beginning you laid the foundations of the earth, *
and the heavens are the work of your hands;

27   'They shall perish, but you will endure; *
they all shall wear out like a garment.

28   'You change them like clothing, and they shall be changed; *
but you are the same, and your years shall not fail.

29   'The children of your servants shall dwell in peace, *
and their descendants shall be established in your sight.'

PSALM 103

1   Bless the Lord, O my soul, *
    and all that is within me, bless his holy name.

2   Bless the Lord, O my soul, *
    and forget not all his benefits;

3   Who forgives all your sins *
    and heals all your infirmities;

4   Who redeems your life from the Pit *
    and crowns you with faithful love and compassion;

5   Who satisfies your days with good things, *
    so that your youth is renewed as an eagle's.

6   The Lord executes righteousness *
    and judgement for all who are oppressed.

7   He made his ways known to Moses *
    and his works to the children of Israel.

8   The Lord is full of compassion and mercy, *
    slow to anger and of great kindness.

9   He will not always accuse us, *
    neither will he keep his anger for ever.

10 He has not dealt with us according to our sins, *
    nor rewarded us according to our wickedness.

11 For as the heavens are high above the earth, *
    so great is his mercy upon those who fear him.

12 As far as the east is from the west, *
    so far has he set our sins from us.

13 As a father has compassion on his children, *
    so is the Lord merciful towards those who fear him.

14 For he knows of what we are made; *
    he remembers that we are but dust.

15   Our days are but as grass; *
     we flourish as a flower of the field;

16   As soon as the wind goes over it, it is gone, *
     and its place shall know it no more.

17   But the merciful goodness of the Lord is from of old
         and endures for ever on those who fear him, *
     and his righteousness on children's children;

18   On those who keep his covenant *
     and remember his commandments to do them.

19   The Lord has established his throne in heaven, *
     and his kingdom has dominion over all.

20   Bless the Lord, you angels of his, *
     you mighty ones who do his bidding,
         and hearken to the voice of his word.

21   Bless the Lord, all you his hosts, *
     you ministers of his who do his will.

22   Bless the Lord, all you works of his,
         in all places of his dominion; *
     bless the Lord, O my soul.

PSALM 104

1   Bless the Lord, O my soul; *
    O Lord my God, you are revealed in glory.

2   You are clothed with majesty and honour, *
    wrapped in light as with a garment.

3   You spread out the heavens like a curtain *
    and lay the beams of your dwelling-place in the waters above.

4   You make the clouds your chariot; *
    and ride on the wings of the wind.

5 You make the winds your messengers *
   and flames of fire your servants.

6 You laid the foundations of the earth, *
   that it never should move at any time.

7 The deep covered it like a garment; *
   the waters stood high above the hills.

8 At your rebuke they fled; *
   at the voice of your thunder they hastened away.

9 They rose up to the hills and flowed down to the valleys beneath, *
   to the place which you had appointed for them.

10 You have set them their bounds that they should not pass; *
    nor turn again to cover the earth.

11 You send the springs into the brooks; *
    which run among the hills.

12 They give drink to every beast of the field *
    and the wild asses quench their thirst.

13 Beside them the birds of the air make their nests *
    and sing among the branches.

14 You water the hills from your dwelling on high; *
    the earth is filled with the fruit of your works.

15 You make grass to grow for the cattle *
    and green plants for the service of all;

16 To bring forth food from the earth, *
    and wine to gladden their hearts,

17 Oil to give them a cheerful countenance, *
    and bread to strengthen their heart.

18 The trees of the Lord are full of sap, *
    the cedars of Lebanon which he planted,

19 In which the birds build their nests, *
    while the fir-trees are a dwelling for the stork.

20 The mountains are a refuge for the wild goats, *
    and the stony cliffs for the conies.

21 You appointed the moon to mark the seasons, *
    and the sun knows the time for its setting.

22 You make darkness that it may be night, *
    in which all the beasts of the forest creep forth.

23 The lions roar for their prey *
    and seek their food from God.

24 The sun rises and they are gone *
    to lay themselves down in their dens.

25 Then the people go forth to their work *
    and to their labour until the evening.

26 O Lord, how manifold are your works! *
    In wisdom you have made them all;
        the earth is full of your creatures.

27 There is the sea, spread far and wide, *
    and there move creatures beyond number, both small and great.

28 There go the ships, and there is that Leviathan, *
    whom you have made to play there.

29 All of these look to you *
    to give them their food in due season.

30 When you give it them, they gather it; *
    you open your hand and they are filled with good.

31 When you hide your face they are troubled; *
    when you take away their breath,
        they die and return again to the dust.

32 When you send forth your spirit, they are created; *
    and you renew the face of the earth.

33 May the glory of the Lord endure for ever; *
    may the Lord rejoice in his works;

34 He looks on the earth and it trembles; *
    he touches the mountains and they smoke.

35 I will sing to the Lord as long as I live; *
    I will make music to my God while I have my being.

36 So shall my song please him *
    while I rejoice in the Lord.

37 Let sinners be consumed out of the earth *
    and the wicked be no more.

38 Bless the Lord, O my soul. *
    Alleluia!

PSALM 105

1 O give thanks to the Lord and proclaim his name; *
   make known his deeds among the peoples.

2 Sing to him, sing praises, *
   and tell of all his marvellous works.

3 Rejoice in the praise of his holy name; *
   let the hearts of them rejoice who seek the Lord.

4 Seek the Lord and his strength; *
   seek his face continually.

5 Remember the marvels he has done, *
   his wonders and the judgements of his mouth,

6 O seed of Abraham his servant, *
   O children of Jacob his chosen.

7 He is the Lord our God; *
   his judgements are in all the earth.

8 He has always been mindful of his covenant, *
   the promise that he made for a thousand generations:

9 The covenant he made with Abraham, *
   the oath that he swore to Isaac,

10 Which he established as a statute for Jacob, *
an everlasting covenant for Israel,

11 Saying, 'To you will I give the land of Canaan *
to be the portion of your inheritance.'

12 When they were but few in number, *
of little account, and sojourners in the land,

13 Wandering from nation to nation, *
from one kingdom to another,

14 He suffered no one to do them wrong *
and rebuked even kings for their sake,

15 Saying, 'Touch not my anointed *
and do my prophets no harm.'

16 Then he called down famine over the land *
and broke every staff of bread.

17 But he had sent a man before them, *
Joseph, who was sold as a slave.

18 They shackled his feet with fetters; *
his neck was ringed with iron.

19 Until all he foretold came to pass, *
the word of the Lord tested him.

20 The king sent and released him; *
the ruler of peoples set him free.

21 He appointed him lord of his household, *
and ruler of all he possessed,

22 To instruct his princes as he willed *
and to teach his counsellors wisdom.

23 Then Israel came into Egypt; *
Jacob sojourned in the land of Ham.

24 And the Lord made his people exceedingly fruitful; *
 he made them too many for their adversaries;

25 Whose heart he turned, so that they hated his people, *
 and dealt craftily with his servants.

26 Then sent he Moses his servant, *
 and Aaron whom he had chosen.

27 He showed his signs through their word *
 and his wonders in the land of Ham.

28 He sent darkness and it grew dark; *
 yet they did not heed his words.

29 He turned their waters into blood *
 and slew all their fish.

30 Their land swarmed with frogs, *
 even in their kings' chambers.

31 He spoke the word, and there came clouds of flies, *
 swarms of gnats within all their borders.

32 He gave them hailstones for rain, *
 and flames of lightning in their land.

33 He blasted their vines and their fig trees *
 and shattered trees across their country.

34 He spoke the word, and the grasshoppers came, *
 and young locusts without number;

35 They ate every plant in their land *
 and devoured the fruit of their soil.

36 He smote all the first-born in their land, *
 the first-fruits of all their strength.

37 Then he brought them out with silver and gold; *
 there was not one among their tribes that stumbled.

38 Egypt was glad at their departing, *
    for a dread of them had fallen upon them.

39 He spread out a cloud for a covering *
    and a fire to light up the night.

40 They asked and he brought them quails, *
    and with the bread of heaven he satisfied them.

41 He opened the rock, and the waters gushed out, *
    and ran in the dry places like a river.

42 For he remembered his holy word, *
    and Abraham, his servant.

43 So he brought forth his people with joy, *
    his chosen ones with singing.

44 He gave them the lands of the nations, *
    and they took possession of the fruit of their toil,

45 That they might keep his statutes *
    and faithfully observe his laws.
        Alleluia!

PSALM 106

1   Alleluia!
        Give thanks to the Lord, for he is gracious, *
    for his faithfulness endures for ever.

2   Who can express the mighty acts of the Lord *
    or show forth all his praise?

3   Happy are those who treasure what is right *
    and always do what is just!

4   Remember me, O Lord, in the favour you bear for your people; *
    visit me in the day of your salvation;

5   That I may see the prosperity of your chosen
        and rejoice in the gladness of your people, *
    and exult with your inheritance.

6   We have sinned like our forebears; *
    we have done wrong and dealt wickedly.

7   In Egypt they did not consider your wonders,
        nor remember the abundance of your faithful love; *
    they rebelled against the Most High at the Red Sea.

8   But he saved them for his name's sake, *
    that he might make his power to be known.

9   He rebuked the Red Sea and it was dried up; *
    so he led them through the deep as through the wilderness.

10 He saved them from the adversary's hand *
    and redeemed them from the hand of the enemy.

11 As for those that troubled them, the waters overwhelmed them; *
    there was not one of them left.

12 Then they believed his words *
    and sang aloud his praise.

13 But soon they forgot his deeds *
    and would not wait for his counsel.

14 A craving seized them in the wilderness, *
    and they put God to the test in the desert.

15 He gave them their desire, *
    but sent a wasting sickness among them.

16 They grew jealous of Moses in the camp, *
    and of Aaron, the holy one of the Lord.

17 So the earth opened and swallowed up Dathan *
    and covered the company of Abiram.

18 A fire was kindled in their company, *
    the flame burnt up the wicked.

19 They made a calf at Horeb *
    and worshipped the molten image;

20 Thus they exchanged their glory *
    for the image of an ox that feeds on hay.

21 They forgot God their saviour, *
   who had done such great things in Egypt,

22 Wonderful deeds in the land of Ham, *
   and fearful things at the Red Sea.

23 So he would have destroyed them,
      had not Moses his chosen stood before him in the breach, *
   to turn away his wrath from consuming them.

24 Then they scorned the promised land *
   and would not believe his word;

25 But murmured in their tents *
   and would not heed the voice of the Lord.

26 So he lifted his hand against them, *
   and swore to overthrow them in the wilderness,

27 To cast out their seed among the nations, *
   and to scatter them throughout the lands.

28 They joined themselves to the Baal of Peor *
   and ate sacrifices offered to the dead.

29 They provoked him to anger with their evil deeds, *
   and a plague broke out among them.

30 Then Phinehas stood up and executed judgement, *
   and so the plague was stayed.

31 This was counted to him for righteousness *
   throughout all generations for ever.

32 They angered him also at the waters of Meribah, *
   so that Moses suffered for their sake;

33 For they so embittered his spirit *
   that he spoke rash words with his lips.

34 They did not destroy the peoples *
   as the Lord had commanded them.

35 They mingled with the nations *
   and learned to follow their ways,

36 So that they worshipped their idols, *
which became to them a snare.

37 They sacrificed their sons *
and their daughters to evil spirits.

38 They shed innocent blood, *
the blood of their sons and daughters,

39 Which they offered to the idols of Canaan, *
and the land was defiled with blood.

40 Thus were they polluted by their actions *
and in their wanton deeds went whoring after other gods.

41 Therefore was the wrath of the Lord
    kindled against his people *
and he abhorred his inheritance.

42 He gave them over to the hand of the nations, *
and those who hated them ruled over them.

43 So their enemies oppressed them, *
and put them in subjection under their hand.

44 Many a time did he deliver them,
    but they rebelled through their own devices, *
and were brought down through their wickedness.

45 Nevertheless, he saw their adversity, *
when he heard their lamentation.

46 He remembered his covenant with them *
and relented according to the greatness of his faithful love.

47 He made them also to be pitied *
by all who had taken them captive.

48 Save us, O Lord our God,
    and gather us from among the nations, *
that we may give thanks to your holy name
    and glory in your praise.

49   Blessèd be the Lord, the God of Israel,
       from everlasting and to everlasting; *
    and let all the people say, Amen!
       Alleluia!

PSALM 107

1   O give thanks to the Lord, for he is gracious, *
    for his steadfast love endures for ever.

2   So let the redeemed of the Lord proclaim *
    even those he redeemed from the hand of the enemy,

3   And gathered out of the lands
       from the east and from the west, *
    from the north and from the south.

4   Some went astray in the wilderness *
    and found no way to a city to dwell in.

5   Hungry and thirsty; *
    their soul was fainting within them.

6   So they cried to the Lord in their trouble, *
    and he delivered them from their distress.

7   He set their feet on the right way *
    till they came to a city to dwell in.

8   *Let them give thanks to the Lord for his goodness* *
    and declare the wonders that he does for his creatures.

9   *For he satisfies the longing soul* *
    and fills the hungry soul with goodness.

10   Some sat in darkness and in the shadow of death, *
    bound fast in misery and iron;

11   For they had rebelled against the words of God *
    and despised the counsel of the Most High.

12 So he bowed down their heart with heaviness; *
   they stumbled and there was none to help them.

13 Then they cried to the Lord in their trouble, *
   and he delivered them from their distress.

14 He brought them out of darkness and out of the shadow of death *
   and broke their bonds asunder.

15 *Let them give thanks to the Lord for his goodness* *
   and declare the wonders that he does for his creatures.

16 *For he has broken the doors of bronze* *
   and breaks the bars of iron in pieces.

17 Some were foolish and took a rebellious way; *
   and were plagued because of their wrongdoing.

18 Their soul abhorred all manner of food *
   and drew near to the gates of death.

19 Then they cried to the Lord in their trouble, *
   and he delivered them from their distress.

20 He sent forth his word and healed them *
   and saved them from destruction.

21 *Let them give thanks to the Lord for his goodness* *
   and declare the wonders that he does for his creatures.

22 *Let them offer him sacrifices of thanksgiving* *
   and tell of his acts with shouts of joy.

23 Those who go down to the sea in ships *
   and do their business in great waters;

24 These have seen the work of the Lord *
   and his wonders in the deep.

25 For at his word the stormy wind arose, *
   and lifted up the waves of the sea.

26   They were carried up to the heavens
        and down again to the deep; *
     their soul melted away in their peril.

27   They reeled and staggered like a drunkard *
     and were at their wits' end.

28   Then they cried to the Lord in their trouble, *
     and he brought them out of their distress.

29   He made the storm be still *
     and the waves of the sea were calmed.

30   Then were they glad because they were at rest; *
     and he brought them to the haven that they desired.

31   *Let them give thanks to the Lord for his goodness ***
     and declare the wonders that he does for his creatures.

32   *Let them exalt him in the congregation of the people ***
     and praise him in the council of the elders.

33   The Lord turns rivers into wilderness, *
     and water-springs into thirsty ground,

34   A fruitful land he makes a salty waste, *
     because of the wickedness of those who dwell there.

35   He makes the wilderness a pool of water *
     and water-springs out of a thirsty land.

36   There he settles the hungry, *
     and they build a city to dwell in.

37   They sow fields and plant vineyards, *
     and bring in a fruitful harvest.

38   He blesses them, so that they multiply greatly; *
     he does not let their herds of cattle decrease.

39   Yet when they are diminished and brought low, *
     through oppression, misfortune or sorrow,

40　He raises the poor from their misery *
　　and multiplies their families like flocks of sheep.

41　He pours contempt on princes *
　　and makes them wander in trackless wastes.

42　The upright will see this and rejoice, *
　　but all wickedness will shut its mouth.

43　Whoever is wise will ponder these things, *
　　and consider the loving-kindness of the Lord.

PSALM 108

1　My heart is ready, O God, my heart is ready; *
　　I will sing and give you praise.

2　Awake, my soul; awake, lyre and harp, *
　　that I may awaken the dawn.

3　I will give you thanks, O Lord, among the peoples; *
　　I will sing praise to you among the nations.

4　For your loving-kindness reaches to the heavens, *
　　and your truth unto the clouds.

5　Be exalted, O God, above the heavens, *
　　and your glory over all the earth.

6　That your beloved may be delivered, *
　　save with your right hand and answer me.

7　God has spoken from his holy place: *
　　'I will triumph and divide Shechem,
　　　　and share out the valley of Succoth.

8　'Gilead is mine and Manasseh is mine; *
　　Ephraim is my helmet and Judah my sceptre.

9　'Moab shall be my wash-pot,
　　　　over Edom will I cast my sandal, *
　　across Philistia will I shout in triumph.'

10   Who will lead me into the strong city? *
      who will bring me into Edom?

11   Have you not cast us off, O God? *
      will you not go forth with our hosts?

12   O grant us your help against the enemy, *
      for earthly help is in vain.

13   Through God will we do great acts, *
      for it is he that shall tread down our enemies.

PSALM 109

1   Keep silent no longer, O God of my praise; *
      for the mouth of wickedness and treachery
        have they opened against me.

2   They have spoken against me with a lying tongue; *
      they encompassed me with words of hatred
        and fought against me without a cause.

3   In return for my love, they set themselves against me; *
      even though I had prayed for them.

4   Thus have they repaid me with evil for good, *
      and hatred for my good will.

5   Appoint a wicked man over him, *
      and let an accuser stand at his right hand.

6   When he is judged, let him be found guilty, *
      and let his prayer be in vain.

7   Let his days be few, *
      and let another take his office.

8   Let his children be fatherless, *
      and his wife become a widow.

9   Let his children wander to beg their bread; *
      let them seek it in desolate places.

10 Let the creditor seize all that he has; *
    let strangers plunder the fruit of his toil.

11 Let there be no one to keep faith with him, *
    or have compassion on his fatherless children.

12 Let his line soon come to an end, *
    and his name be blotted out in the next generation.

13 Let the wickedness of his fathers
        be remembered before the Lord, *
    and no sin of his mother be blotted out;

14 Let their sin be always before the Lord; *
    that he may root out their name from the earth;

15 Because he was not minded to keep faith, *
    but persecuted the poor and needy
        and sought to kill the brokenhearted.

16 He loved cursing and it came to him; *
    he took no delight in blessing and it was far from him.

17 He clothed himself with cursing as with a garment: *
    it seeped into his body like water
        and into his bones like oil;

18 Let it be to him like the cloak
        which he wraps around him, *
    and like the belt that he wears continually.

19 Thus may the Lord repay my accusers, *
    and those who speak evil against me.

20 But deal with me, O Lord my God, according to your name; *
    O deliver me, for sweet is your faithfulness.

21 For I am helpless and poor, *
    and my heart is wounded within me.

22 I fade like a shadow that lengthens; *
    I am driven away like a locust.

23 My knees are weak through fasting, *
    and my flesh is dried up and wasted.

24 I have become a reproach to them; *
    those who see me shake their heads in scorn.

25 Help me, O Lord my God; *
    save me for your loving mercy's sake.

26 And they shall know that this is your hand, *
    that you, O Lord, have done it.

27 Though they curse, yet will you bless; *
    let those who rise up against me be confounded,
        but let your servant rejoice.

28 Let my accusers be clothed with disgrace *
    and wrap themselves in their shame as in a cloak.

29 I will give great thanks to the Lord with my mouth; *
    in the midst of the multitude will I praise him;

30 Because he has stood at the right hand of the needy, *
    to save my soul from those who would condemn.

PSALM 110

1   The Lord said to my lord, 'Sit at my right hand, *
    until I make your enemies your footstool.'

2   May the Lord stretch forth the sceptre of your power; *
    rule from Zion in the midst of your enemies.

3   'Noble are you on this day of your birth; *
    on the holy mountain, from the womb of the dawn
        the dew of your new birth is upon you.'

4   The Lord has sworn and will not recant: *
    'You are a priest for ever after the order of Melchizedek.'

5   The king at your right hand, O Lord, *
    will smite down kings in the day of his wrath.

6 In all his majesty, he will judge among the nations; *
  smiting heads over all the wide earth.

7 He shall drink from the brook by the way; *
  therefore shall he lift high his head.

PSALM 111

1 Alleluia!
  I will give thanks to the Lord with my whole heart, *
  in the company of the faithful and in the congregation.

2 The works of the Lord are great; *
  sought out by all who delight in them.

3 His work is full of majesty and honour, *
  and his righteousness endures for ever.

4 He appointed a memorial for his marvellous deeds; *
  the Lord is gracious and full of compassion.

5 He gave food to those who feared him; *
  he is ever mindful of his covenant.

6 He showed his people the power of his works *
  in giving them the heritage of the nations.

7 The works of his hands are truth and justice; *
  all his commandments are sure.

8 They stand fast for ever and ever; *
  they are done in truth and equity.

9 He sent redemption to his people;
  he commanded his covenant for ever; *
  holy and awesome is his name.

10 The fear of the Lord is the beginning of wisdom;
   a good understanding have those who live by it; *
   his praise endures for ever.

PSALM 112

1   Alleluia!
     Blessed are those who fear the Lord *
     and have great delight in his commandments!

2   Their descendants will be mighty in the land; *
     a generation of the faithful that will be blessed.

3   Wealth and riches will be in their house, *
     and their righteousness endures for ever.

4   Light shines in the darkness for the upright; *
     gracious and full of compassion are the righteous.

5   How happy are those who lend in kindness *
     and order their affairs with justice,

6   For they will never be shaken; *
     the righteous will be held in everlasting remembrance.

7   They will not be afraid of any evil tidings; *
     their heart is steadfast, trusting in the Lord.

8   Their heart is sustained and will not fear, *
     until they see the downfall of their foes.

9   They have given freely to the poor,
         their righteousness stands fast for ever; *
     their horn will be exalted with honour.

10   The wicked shall see it and be angry;
         they shall gnash their teeth in despair; *
     the desire of the wicked shall perish.

PSALM 113

1   Alleluia!
    Praise, O servants of the Lord, *
O praise the name of the Lord.

2   Blessed be the name of the Lord, *
from this time forth and for evermore.

3   From the rising of the sun to its setting *
let the name of the Lord be praised.

4   The Lord is high above all nations, *
and his glory above the heavens.

5   Who is like the Lord our God,
    that has his throne so high, *
yet humbles himself to behold
    the things of heaven and earth?

6   He raises the poor from the dust *
and lifts the needy from the ashes

7   To set them with princes, *
with the princes of his people.

8   He gives the barren woman a place in the house, *
and makes her a joyful mother of children.
    Alleluia!

PSALM 114

1   When Israel came out of Egypt, *
the house of Jacob from a people of a strange tongue,

2   Judah became his sanctuary; *
Israel his dominion.

3   The sea saw that, and fled; *
Jordan was driven back.

4   The mountains skipped like rams; *
the little hills like young sheep.

5 What ails you, O sea, that you flee away? *
  O Jordan, that you turn back?

6 You mountains, that you skip like rams? *
  you little hills like young sheep?

7 Tremble, O earth, at the presence of the Lord, *
  at the presence of the God of Jacob,

8 Who turns the hard rock into a pool of water, *
  the flint-stone into a springing well.

PSALM 115

1 Not to us, Lord, not to us,
   but to your name give the glory; *
  for the sake of your loving mercy and truth.

2 Why should the heathen say, *
  'Where is now their God?'

3 As for our God, he is in heaven; *
  he does whatever he pleases.

4 Their idols are silver and gold, *
  the work of human hands.

5 They have a mouth, but cannot speak; *
  eyes have they, but cannot see;

6 They have ears, but cannot hear; *
  a nose have they, but cannot smell;

7 They have hands, but cannot feel;
   feet have they, but cannot walk; *
  not a whisper do they make from their throat.

8 Those who make them shall become like them, *
  and so will all who put their trust in them.

9 But you, house of Israel, trust in the Lord; *
  he is your help and your shield.

10   O house of Aaron, trust in the Lord; *
     he is your help and your shield.

11   You that fear the Lord, trust in the Lord; *
     he is your help and your shield.

12   The Lord has been mindful of us and he will bless us; *
     may he bless the house of Israel;
       may he bless the house of Aaron;

13   May he bless those who fear the Lord, *
     both small and great together.

14   May the Lord increase you more and more, *
     you and your children after you.

15   May you be blessed by the Lord, *
     the maker of heaven and earth.

16   The heavens are the heavens of the Lord, *
     but the earth has he entrusted to its peoples.

17   The dead do not praise the Lord, *
     nor those gone down into silence;

18   But we will bless the Lord, *
     from this time forth for evermore.
       Alleluia!

PSALM 116

1   I love the Lord,
     for he has heard the voice of my supplication; *
   he inclined his ear to me
     on the day that I called out to him.

2   The snares of death encompassed me;
     the pains of hell took hold of me; *
   by grief and sorrow was I held.

3   Then I called upon the name of the Lord: *
   'O Lord, I beg you, deliver my soul.'

4   Gracious is the Lord and righteous; *
       our God is full of compassion.

5   The Lord watches over the simple; *
       I was brought very low and he saved me.

6   Turn again to your rest, O my soul, *
       for the Lord has been gracious to you.

7   For you have delivered my soul from death, *
       my eyes from tears and my feet from falling.

8   I will walk before the Lord *
       in the land of the living.

9   I believed that I should perish
       for I was sorely troubled; *
    and I said in my alarm,
       'Everyone is a liar.'

10   How shall I repay the Lord *
       for all the benefits he has given to me?

11   I will lift up the cup of salvation *
       and call upon the name of the Lord.

12   I will fulfil my vows to the Lord *
       in the presence of all his people.

13   Precious in the sight of the Lord *
       is the death of his faithful servants.

14   O Lord, I am your servant; *
       your servant, the child of your handmaid;
         you have freed me from my bonds.

15   I will offer to you a sacrifice of thanksgiving *
       and proclaim the name of the Lord.

16   I will fulfil my vows to the Lord *
       in the presence of all his people.

17   In the courts of the house of the Lord, *
       in the midst of you, O Jerusalem.
          Alleluia!

PSALM 117

1   O praise the Lord, all you nations; *
      praise him, all you peoples.

2   For his faithful love towers over us, *
      and the truth of the Lord endures for ever.
        Alleluia!

PSALM 118

1   O give thanks to the Lord, for he is good; *
      his mercy endures for ever.

2   Let Israel now proclaim, *
      'His mercy endures for ever.'

3   Let the house of Aaron now proclaim, *
      'His mercy endures for ever.'

4   Let those who fear the Lord proclaim, *
      'His mercy endures for ever.'

5   In my constraint, I called to the Lord; *
      the Lord answered and set me free.

6   The Lord is at my side; I will not fear; *
      what can flesh do to me?

7   With the Lord at my side as my saviour; *
      I shall see the downfall of my enemies.

8   It is better to take refuge in the Lord *
      than to put any confidence in flesh.

9   It is better to take refuge in the Lord *
      than to put any confidence in princes.

10   All the nations encompassed me; *
     but by the name of the Lord I drove them back.

11   They hemmed me in, they hemmed me in on every side; *
     but by the name of the Lord I drove them back.

12   They swarmed about me like bees;
        they blazed like fire among thorns; *
     but by the name of the Lord I drove them back.

13   You thrust me, you thrust me to the brink, *
     but the Lord came to my help.

14   The Lord is my strength and my song, *
     and he has become my salvation.

15   Hear the joyful shouts of salvation, *
     rising from the tents of the righteous:

16   'The right hand of the Lord does mighty deeds; *
     the right hand of the Lord raises up;
        the right hand of the Lord does mighty deeds.'

17   I shall not die, but live, *
     and declare the works of the Lord.

18   The Lord has punished me sorely, *
     but he has not given me over to death.

19   Open to me the gates of righteousness; *
     that I may enter and give thanks to the Lord.

20   This is the gate of the Lord; *
     the righteous shall enter through it.

21   I will give thanks to you, for you have answered me *
     and have become my salvation.

22   The stone which the builders rejected *
     has become the chief corner-stone.

23   This is the Lord's doing, *
    and it is marvellous in our eyes.

24   This is the day that the Lord has made; *
    we will rejoice and be glad in it.

25   Come, O Lord, and save us we pray. *
    Come, Lord, send us now prosperity.

26   Blessèd be he who comes in the name of the Lord; *
    we bless you from the house of the Lord.

27   The Lord is God; he has given us light; *
    bind the festal dance with cords
      up to the horns of the altar.

28   You are my God and I will thank you; *
    you are my God and I will exalt you.

29   O give thanks to the Lord, for he is good; *
    his mercy endures for ever.

PSALM 119

1 Aleph

1   Happy are they whose way is pure, *
    who walk in the law of the Lord!

2   Happy are they who keep his testimonies *
    and seek him with all their hearts!

3   Those who do no wickedness, *
    but walk in his ways.

4   You, O Lord, have commanded *
    that we should diligently keep your precepts.

5   O that my ways were made so direct *
    that I might keep your statutes!

6 Then I should not be put to shame, *
   when I regard all your commandments.

7 I will thank you with an unfeigned heart, *
   when I have learned your righteous judgements.

8 I will keep your statutes; *
   O forsake me not utterly.

   2 Beth

9 How shall the young cleanse their way? *
   even by ruling themselves according to your word.

10 With my whole heart have I sought you; *
   O let me not go astray from your commandments.

11 Your words have I hidden within my heart, *
   that I should not sin against you.

12 Blessèd are you, O Lord; *
   O teach me your statutes.

13 With my lips have I been telling *
   of all the judgements of your mouth.

14 I have taken greater delight in the way of your testimonies *
   than in all manner of riches.

15 I will meditate on your commandments *
   and contemplate your ways.

16 My delight shall be in your statutes; *
   and I will not forget your word.

   3 Gimel

17 O do good to your servant that I may live, *
   and so shall I keep your word.

18 Open my eyes, that I may see *
   the wonders of your law.

19   I am a stranger upon earth; *
     hide not your commandments from me.

20   My soul is consumed at all times *
     with fervent longing for your judgements.

21   You have rebuked the arrogant; *
     cursed are those who stray from your commandments!

22   Turn from me shame and rebuke, *
     for I have kept your testimonies.

23   Rulers also sit and speak against me, *
     but your servant meditates on your statutes.

24   For your testimonies are my delight; *
     they are my faithful counsellors.

     4 *Daleth*

25   My soul cleaves to the dust; *
     O give me life according to your word.

26   I have examined my ways and you have answered me; *
     O teach me your statutes.

27   Make me to understand the way of your commandments, *
     and so shall I meditate on your wondrous works.

28   My soul melts away in tears of sorrow; *
     raise me up according to your word.

29   Take from me the way of falsehood; *
     be gracious to me through your law.

30   I have chosen the way of truth; *
     and your judgements have I laid before me.

31   I hold fast to your testimonies; *
     O Lord, let me not be put to shame.

32   I will run the way of your commandments, *
     when you have set my heart at liberty.

5 He

33 Teach me, O Lord, the way of your statutes, *
and I shall keep it to the end.

34 Give me understanding and I shall keep your law; *
I shall keep it with all my heart.

35 Lead me in the path of your commandments, *
for therein is my delight.

36 Incline my heart to your testimonies *
and not to unjust gain.

37 Turn away my eyes lest they gaze on vanities; *
O give me life in your way.

38 Confirm to your servant your promise, *
which stands for all who fear you.

39 Turn away the reproach which I dread, *
because your judgements are good.

40 Behold, I long for your commandments; *
in your righteousness give me life.

6 Waw

41 Let your faithful love come to me, O Lord, *
even your salvation, according to your promise.

42 Then shall I answer those who taunt me, *
for my trust is in your word.

43 O take not the word of truth utterly out of my mouth, *
for my hope is in your judgements.

44 So shall I always keep your law; *
I shall keep it for ever and ever.

45 I will walk at liberty, *
because I study your commandments.

46 I will tell of your testimonies also, even before kings *
    and will not be ashamed.

47 My delight shall be in your commandments, *
    which I have greatly loved.

48 My hands will I lift up to your commandments
        which I love, *
    and I will meditate on your statutes.

    7 Zayin

49 Remember your word to your servant, *
    on which you have built my hope.

50 This is my comfort in my trouble, *
    that your promise gives me life.

51 The proud have derided me cruelly, *
    but I have not turned aside from your law.

52 I have remembered your everlasting judgements, O Lord, *
    and so have I been comforted.

53 I am seized with horror at the wicked, *
    for they have forsaken your law.

54 Your statutes have been like songs to me *
    in the house of my pilgrimage.

55 I have thought on your name in the night, O Lord, *
    and so have I kept your law.

56 These blessings have been mine, *
    for I have kept your commandments.

    8 Heth

57 You only are my portion, O Lord; *
    I have promised to keep your words.

58 I entreat you with all my heart, *
    be merciful to me according to your promise.

59 I have considered my ways *
and turned my feet to your testimonies.

60 I made haste and did not delay *
to keep your commandments.

61 Though the cords of the wicked entangle me, *
I do not forget your law.

62 At midnight I will rise to give you thanks, *
because of your righteous judgements.

63 I am a companion of all who fear you, *
to those who keep your commandments.

64 The earth, O Lord, is full of your faithful love; *
instruct me in your statutes.

9 Teth

65 You have dealt graciously with your servant, *
according to your word, O Lord.

66 O teach me true understanding and knowledge, *
for I have trusted in your commandments.

67 Before I was afflicted I went astray, *
but now I keep your word.

68 You are good and gracious; *
O Lord, teach me your statutes.

69 The proud have smeared me with lies, *
but I will keep your commandments with my whole heart.

70 Their heart has become gross as fat, *
but my delight is in your law.

71 It is good for me that I have been afflicted, *
that I might learn your statutes.

72 The law of your mouth is dearer to me *
than thousands of gold and silver pieces.

10 Yodh

73 Your hands have made me and fashioned me; *
give me understanding, that I may learn your commandments.

74 Those who fear you will be glad when they see me, *
because I put my hope in your word.

75 I know, O Lord, that your judgements are right *
and that in very faithfulness you caused me to be troubled.

76 Let your faithful love be my comfort *
according to your promise to your servant.

77 Let your tender mercies come to me, that I may live, *
for your law is my delight.

78 Let the proud be put to shame, for they wrong me with lies; *
but I will meditate on your commandments.

79 Let those who fear you turn to me, *
even those who know your testimonies.

80 Let my heart be sound in your statutes, *
that I may not be put to shame.

11 Kaph

81 My soul has longed for your salvation; *
I have put my hope in your word.

82 My eyes fail with watching for your word, *
while I say, 'O when will you comfort me?'

83 I have become like a bottle in the smoke, *
yet I do not forget your statutes.

84 How many are the days of your servant? *
O when will you bring judgement on those who persecute me?

85 The proud have dug pits for me; *
they do not keep your law.

86 All your commandments are true; *
   O help me, for they persecute me with falsehood.

87 They had almost made an end of me on earth, *
   but I have not forsaken your commandments.

88 Give me life according to your loving-kindness; *
   so shall I keep the testimonies of your mouth.

   12 Lamedh

89 O Lord, your word is everlasting; *
   it ever stands firm in the heavens.

90 Your faithfulness also remains from one generation to another; *
   you have established the earth and it abides.

91 So also your judgements stand firm this day, *
   for all things are your servants.

92 If your law had not been my delight, *
   I should have perished in my trouble.

93 I will never forget your commandments, *
   because by them you give me new life.

94 I am yours, O save me! *
   for I have sought your commandments.

95 The wicked have waited for me to destroy me, *
   but I will meditate on your testimonies.

96 I have seen an end of all perfection, *
   but your commandment has no bounds.

   13 Mem

97 Lord, how I love your law! *
   All the day long it is my meditation.

98 Your commandment has made me wiser than my enemies, *
   for it is ever with me.

99 I have more understanding than all my teachers, *
  for your testimonies are my meditation.

100 I am wiser than the agèd, *
  because I keep your commandments.

101 I restrain my feet from every evil way, *
  that I may keep your word.

102 I have not turned aside from your judgements, *
  for you have been my teacher.

103 How sweet are your words to my tongue! *
  They are sweeter than honey to my mouth.

104 Through your commandments I get understanding; *
  therefore I hate all evil ways.

  14 Num

105 Your word is a lantern to my feet *
  and a light upon my path.

106 I have sworn and will fulfill it, *
  that I shall keep your righteous judgements.

107 I am troubled above measure; *
  give me life, O Lord, according to your word.

108 Accept the free-will offering of my mouth, O Lord, *
  and teach me your judgements.

109 My soul is ever in my hand, *
  yet I do not forget your law.

110 The wicked have laid a snare for me, *
  but I have not strayed from your commandments.

111 Your testimonies have I claimed as my heritage for ever; *
  for they are the very joy of my heart.

112 I have applied my heart to fulfil your statutes *
  always, even to the end.

15 Samekh

113 I hate those who are double-minded, *
but your law do I love.

114 You are my hiding-place and my shield; *
and my hope is in your word.

115 Away from me, you wicked. *
I will keep the commandments of my God.

116 Sustain me according to your promise, that I may live, *
and let me not be disappointed in my hope.

117 Hold me up and I shall be saved, *
and my delight shall be ever in your statutes.

118 You set at nought those who depart from your statutes; *
for their deceiving is in vain.

119 You consider all the wicked as dross; *
therefore I love your testimonies.

120 My flesh trembles for fear of you; *
and I am afraid of your judgements.

16 Ayin

121 I have done what is just and right; *
O give me not over to my oppressors.

122 Stand surety for your servant's good; *
let not the proud oppress me.

123 My eyes fail with watching for your salvation *
and for your righteous promise.

124 O deal with your servant according to your faithful love *
and teach me your statutes.

125 I am your servant; O grant me understanding, *
that I may know your testimonies.

126 It is time for you to act, O Lord, *
   for they frustrate your law.

127 Truly, I love your commandments *
   above gold, even much fine gold.

128 Therefore I hold all your commandments dear; *
   and all false ways I utterly abhor.

   17 Pe

129 Your testimonies are wonderful; *
   therefore my soul keeps them.

130 The opening of your word gives light; *
   it gives understanding to the simple.

131 I open my mouth and draw in my breath *
   as I long for your commandments.

132 O turn to me and have mercy upon me, *
   according to your judgement for those who love your name.

133 Order my steps by your word; *
   and let no wickedness have dominion over me.

134 Redeem me from earthly oppressors *
   so that I may keep your commandments.

135 Show the light of your countenance upon your servant *
   and teach me your statutes.

136 My eyes run down with streams of water, *
   because they do not keep your law.

   18 Tsade

137 Righteous are you, O Lord, *
   and true are your judgements.

138 You have appointed your decrees in righteousness *
   and in great faithfulness.

139 My indignation consumes me, *
     because my adversaries forget your word.

140 Your word has been tried to the uttermost, *
     and therefore your servant loves it.

141 I am small and of no reputation, *
     yet do I not forget your commandments.

142 Your righteousness is an everlasting righteousness *
     and your law is the truth.

143 Trouble and heaviness have taken hold upon me, *
     yet my delight is in your commandments.

144 The righteousness of your testimonies is everlasting; *
     O grant me understanding and I shall live.

19 Qoph

145 I call with my whole heart; *
     answer me, O Lord, that I may keep your statutes.

146 To you I call, O save me! *
     and I shall keep your testimonies.

147 Early in the morning I cry to you, *
     for in your word is my trust.

148 My eyes are open before the night-watches, *
     that I may meditate on your word.

149 Hear my voice, O Lord, according to your faithful love; *
     according to your judgements, give me life.

150 They draw near who in malice persecute me; *
     but they are far from your law.

151 You, O Lord, are near at hand, *
     and all your commandments are true.

152 Long have I known of your testimonies, *
     that you have founded them for ever.

20 Resh

153 O consider my affliction and deliver me, *
     for I do not forget your law.

154 Plead my cause and redeem me; *
     according to your promise, give me life.

155 Salvation is far from the wicked, *
     for they do not seek your statutes.

156 Great is your compassion, O Lord; *
     give me life, according to your judgements.

157 Many there are that persecute and oppress me, *
     yet do I not swerve from your testimonies.

158 It grieves me when I see the treacherous, *
     for they do not keep your word.

159 Consider, O Lord, how I love your commandments *
     give me life according to your loving-kindness.

160 The sum of your word is truth *
     and all your righteous judgements endure for evermore.

21 Shin

161 Princes have persecuted me without a cause, *
     but my heart stands in awe of your word.

162 I am as glad of your word *
     as one who finds great spoils.

163 As for lies, I hate and abhor them, *
     but your law do I love.

164 Seven times a day do I praise you, *
     because of your righteous judgements.

165 Great peace have they who love your law; *
     and they shall not be overthrown.

166 Lord, I have looked for your salvation *
   and I have fulfilled your commandments.

167 My soul has kept your testimonies *
   and greatly have I loved them.

168 I have kept your commandments and testimonies, *
   for all my ways are before you.

   22 Taw

169 Let my cry come before you, O Lord; *
   give me understanding, according to your word.

170 Let my supplication come before you; *
   deliver me, according to your promise.

171 My lips shall pour forth your praise, *
   when you have taught me your statutes.

172 My tongue shall sing of your word, *
   for all your commandments are righteous.

173 Let your hand reach out to help me, *
   for I have chosen your commandments.

174 I have longed for your salvation, O Lord, *
   and your law is my delight.

175 Let my soul live and it shall praise you, *
   and let your judgements be my help.

176 I have gone astray like a sheep that is lost; *
   O seek your servant, for I do not forget your commandments.

PSALM 120

1   When I was in trouble I called to the Lord, *
     I called to the Lord and he answered me.

2   Deliver me, O Lord, from lying lips *
     and from a deceitful tongue.

3   What shall be given to you? What more shall be done to you, *
     O you deceitful tongue?

4   The sharp arrows of a warrior, *
     with hot burning coals.

5   Woe is me, that I must lodge in Meshech *
     and dwell among the tents of Kedar!

6   My soul has long dwelt with those *
     that are enemies of peace.

7   I am for making peace, *
     but when I speak of it, they make ready for war.

PSALM 121

1   I lift up my eyes to the hills; *
     from where is my help to come?

2   My help comes from the Lord, *
     the maker of heaven and earth.

3   He will not suffer your foot to stumble *
     he who watches over you will not sleep.

4   Behold, he who keeps watch over Israel *
     shall neither slumber nor sleep;

5   The Lord himself watches over you; *
     the Lord is your shade at your right hand,

6   So that the sun shall not strike you by day, *
     neither the moon by night.

7   The Lord shall keep you from all evil; *
     it is he who shall keep your soul.

8   The Lord shall keep watch over your going out
         and your coming in, *
     from this time forth for evermore.

PSALM 122

1   I was glad when they said to me, *
     'Let us go to the house of the Lord.'

2   And now our feet are standing *
     within your gates, O Jerusalem;

3   Jerusalem, built as a city *
     that is at unity in itself.

4   Thither the tribes go up, the tribes of the Lord, *
     as is the law for Israel, to give thanks to the name of the Lord.

5   For there are the thrones of judgement, *
     the thrones of the house of David.

6   O pray for the peace of Jerusalem: *
     'May they prosper who love you.

7   'Peace be within your walls *
     and tranquillity within your palaces.

8   'For my kindred and companions' sake, *
     I will pray that peace be with you.

9   'For the sake of the house of the Lord our God, *
     I will seek to do you good.'

PSALM 123

1   To you I lift up my eyes, *
     to you who are enthroned in the heavens.

2   As the eyes of servants look to the hand of their master, *
     or the eyes of a maid to the hand of her mistress,

3   So our eyes wait upon the Lord our God, *
     until he have mercy upon us.

4   Have mercy upon us, O Lord, have mercy upon us, *
     for we have had more than enough of contempt,

5   Our soul is filled with the scorn of the arrogant, *
     and with the contempt of the proud.

PSALM 124

1   If the Lord himself had not been on our side, *
     now may Israel say;

2   If the Lord had not been on our side, *
     when enemies rose up against us;

3   Then would they have swallowed us alive *
     when their anger burned against us;

4   Then would the waters have overwhelmed us
     and the torrent gone over our soul; *
     over our soul would have swept the raging waters.

5   But blessèd be the Lord! *
     who has not given us over to be a prey for their teeth.

6   Our soul has escaped
     as a bird from the snare of the fowler; *
     the snare is broken and we are delivered.

7   Our help is in the name of the Lord, *
     who has made heaven and earth.

PSALM 125

1   Those who trust in the Lord are like Mount Zion, *
      which cannot be moved, but stands fast for ever.

2   As the hills stand about Jerusalem; *
      so the Lord stands round about his people,
        from this time forth for evermore.

3   The sceptre of wickedness shall not hold sway
        over the portion given to the righteous, *
      lest the righteous turn their hands to evil.

4   Do good, O Lord, to those who are good *
      and to those who are true of heart.

5   Those who turn aside to crooked ways
        the Lord shall take away with the evildoers; *
      but let there be peace upon Israel.

PSALM 126

1   When the Lord restored the fortunes of Zion, *
      then were we like those who dream.

2   Then was our mouth filled with laughter, *
      and our tongue with songs of joy.

3   Then said they among the nations, *
      The Lord has done great things for them.

4   The Lord has indeed done great things for us *
      and therefore we rejoiced.

5   Restore again our fortunes, O Lord, *
      as the river-beds of the wilderness.

6   Those who sow in tears *
      shall reap with songs of joy.

7   Those who go out weeping, bearing the seed, *
      shall come back singing for joy, bearing home their sheaves.

PSALM 127

1   Except the Lord build the house, *
    those who build it labour in vain.

2   Except the Lord keep the city, *
    the guard keeps watch in vain.

3   It is in vain that you hasten to rise up early
      and go so late to your rest, eating the bread of toil, *
    so he gives his belovèd their sleep.

4   Children are a heritage from the Lord, *
    and the fruit of the womb is his gift.

5   Like arrows in the hand of a warrior *
    so are the children of one's youth.

6   Happy are they who have their quiver full of them! *
    They shall not be put to shame
      when they dispute with their enemies in the gate.

PSALM 128

1   Blessed are all those who fear the Lord, *
    and who walk in his ways!

2   You shall eat the fruit of the labour of your hands; *
    it shall go well with you, and happy shall you be.

3   Your wife shall be like a fruitful vine
      on the walls of your house, *
    your children like the olive shoots
      round about your table.

4   Thus shall the one be blessed *
    who fears the Lord.

5   The Lord from out of Zion bless you, *
    that you may see Jerusalem in prosperity
      all the days of your life.

6   May you see your children's children *
and may there be peace upon Israel.

PSALM 129

1   'Many a time have they fought against me from my youth', *
may Israel now say;

2   'Many a time have they fought against me from my youth, *
but they have not prevailed against me.'

3   The ploughers ploughed upon my back *
and made long their furrows.

4   But the righteous Lord *
has cut the cords of the wicked in pieces.

5   Let them be put to shame and turned backwards, *
as many as are enemies of Zion.

6   Let them be like grass upon the house-tops, *
which withers before it can be plucked;

7   So that no reaper could fill his hand, *
nor a binder of sheaves his bosom.

8   So that none who go by say,
'The blessing of the Lord be upon you.' *
We bless you in the name of the Lord.

PSALM 130

1   Out of the depths I call to you, O Lord;
Lord, hear my voice; *
let your ears consider well the voice of my supplication.

2   If you, Lord, were to mark what is done amiss, *
O Lord, who could stand?

3   But there is forgiveness with you; *
so that you shall be feared.

4   I wait for the Lord; my soul waits for him; *
     in his word is my hope.

5   My soul waits for the Lord,
       more than the night-watch for the morning, *
     more than the night-watch for the morning.

6   O Israel, wait for the Lord, *
     for with the Lord there is mercy;

7   With him is plenteous redemption, *
     and he shall redeem Israel from all their sins.

PSALM 131

1   O Lord, my heart is not proud; *
     my eyes are not raised in haughty looks.

2   I do not occupy myself with great matters, *
     with things that are too great for me.

3   But I have quieted and stilled my soul,
       like a weaned child on its mother; *
     so my soul is quieted within me.

4   O Israel, trust in the Lord, *
     from this time forth for evermore.

PSALM 132

1   Lord, remember for David *
     all the hardships he endured;

2   How he swore an oath to the Lord *
     and vowed a vow to the Mighty One of Jacob:

3   'I will not come within the shelter of my house, *
     nor climb up into my bed;

4   'I will not allow my eyes to sleep, *
     nor let my eyelids slumber;

5   'Until I find a place for the Lord, *
     a dwelling for the Mighty One of Jacob.

6   'Now, we heard of the ark in Ephrata, *
     and found it in the forest.

7   'Let us enter the place of his dwelling, *
     and fall low before his footstool.'

8   Arise, O Lord, into your resting-place, *
     you and the ark of your strength.

9   Let your priests be clothed with righteousness, *
     and your faithful ones sing with joy.

10   For your servant David's sake, *
     turn not away the face of your anointed.

11   The Lord has sworn an oath to David; *
     a promise from which he will not shrink:

12   'Of the fruit of your body *
     shall I set upon your throne.

13   'If your children keep my covenant
       and my testimonies that I shall teach them, *
     their children also shall sit upon your throne for evermore.'

14   For the Lord has chosen Zion for himself, *
     he has desired her for his habitation:

15   'This shall be my resting-place for ever; *
     here will I dwell, for I have longed for her.

16   'I will abundantly bless her provision; *
     her poor will I satisfy with bread.

17   'I will clothe her priests with salvation, *
     and her faithful ones shall rejoice and sing.

18   'There will I make a horn to spring up for David; *
     I will keep a lantern burning for my anointed.

19   'As for his enemies, I will clothe them with shame; *
      but on him shall his crown be bright.'

PSALM 133

1   Behold how good and pleasant it is *
     to dwell together in unity!

2   It is like the precious oil upon the head *
     that ran down upon the beard,

3   Even on Aaron's beard, *
     and ran down upon the collar of his clothing;

4   As though the dew of Hermon *
     ran down on the hills of Zion.

5   For there the Lord has promised his blessing: *
     even life for evermore.

PSALM 134

1   Come, bless the Lord,
     all you servants of the Lord, *
     you that by night stand in the house of the Lord.

2   Lift up your hands towards the holy presence *
     and bless the Lord.

3   The Lord who made heaven and earth *
     give you blessing out of Zion.

PSALM 135

1   Alleluia!
     O praise the name of the Lord; *
    praise it, you servants of the Lord,

2   You that stand in the house of the Lord, *
    in the courts of the house of our God.

3   O praise the Lord, for the Lord is good; *
    make music to his name, for it is gracious.

4   For the Lord has chosen Jacob for himself *
    and Israel for his own possession.

5   For I know that the Lord is great, *
    and that our Lord is above all gods.

6   The Lord does whatever he pleases
        in heaven and on earth, *
    in the seas and in all the deeps.

7   He brings up the clouds from the ends of the earth; *
    he makes lightning with the rain,
        and brings the winds out of his treasures.

8   He smote the first-born of Egypt, *
    the first-born of human and beast.

9   He sent signs and wonders into your midst, O Egypt, *
    upon Pharaoh and all his servants.

10 He smote many nations *
    and slew mighty kings:

11 Sihon, king of the Amorites,
        and Og, the king of Bashan, *
    and all the kings of Canaan.

12 He gave their land as a heritage, *
    a heritage for Israel his people.

13 Your name, O Lord, endures for ever, *
   and shall be remembered through all generations.

14 For the Lord will vindicate his people *
   and have compassion on his servants.

15 The idols of the nations are but silver and gold, *
   the work of human hands.

16 They have a mouth, but cannot speak; *
   eyes have they, but cannot see;

17 They have ears, but cannot hear; *
   neither is there any breath in their mouth.

18 Those who make them shall become like them, *
   and so will all who put their trust in them.

19 Bless the Lord, O house of Israel; *
   O house of Aaron, bless the Lord.

20 Bless the Lord, O house of Levi; *
   you who fear the Lord, bless the Lord.

21 Blessèd be the Lord from Zion, *
   who dwells in Jerusalem.
       Alleluia!

PSALM 136

1 Give thanks to the Lord, for he is gracious; *
   for his mercy endures for ever.

2 Give thanks to the God of gods, *
   for his mercy endures for ever.

3 Give thanks to the Lord of lords, *
   for his mercy endures for ever.

4 Who alone does great wonders, *
   for his mercy endures for ever;

5   Who by wisdom made the heavens, *
for his mercy endures for ever;

6   Who laid out the earth upon the waters, *
for his mercy endures for ever;

7   Who made the great lights, *
for his mercy endures for ever;

8   The sun to rule the day, *
for his mercy endures for ever;

9   The moon and the stars to govern the night, *
for his mercy endures for ever;

10   Who smote the first-born of Egypt, *
for his mercy endures for ever;

11   And brought out Israel from among them, *
for his mercy endures for ever;

12   With a mighty hand and outstretched arm, *
for his mercy endures for ever;

13   Who divided the Red Sea in two, *
for his mercy endures for ever;

14   And made Israel to pass through the midst of it, *
for his mercy endures for ever;

15   But Pharaoh and his host he overthrew in the Red Sea, *
for his mercy endures for ever;

16   Who led his people through the wilderness, *
for his mercy endures for ever;

17   Who smote great kings, *
for his mercy endures for ever;

18   And slew mighty kings, *
for his mercy endures for ever;

19   Sihon, king of the Amorites, *
for his mercy endures for ever;

20 And Og, the king of Bashan, *
for his mercy endures for ever;

21 And gave away their land for a heritage, *
for his mercy endures for ever;

22 A heritage for Israel his servant, *
for his mercy endures for ever;

23 Who remembered us when we were in trouble, *
for his mercy endures for ever;

24 And delivered us from our enemies, *
for his mercy endures for ever;

25 Who gives food to all creatures, *
for his mercy endures for ever;

26 O give thanks to the God of heaven, *
for his mercy endures for ever.

PSALM 137

1 By the waters of Babylon we sat down and wept, *
when we remembered Zion.

2 As for our harps, we hung them up *
on the willows that grow in that land.

3 For those who had taken us captive asked for a song,
    our tormentors called for music: *
'Sing us one of the songs of Zion'.

4 How shall we sing the Lord's song *
in a foreign land?

5 If I forget you, O Jerusalem, *
let my right hand forget its skill.

6 Let my tongue cleave to the roof of my mouth
    if I do not remember you, *
if I set not Jerusalem above my highest joy.

7 Remember, O Lord, against the people of Edom
   the day of Jerusalem *
how they said, 'Down with it! Down with it!
   Even to the ground!'

8 O daughter of Babylon, doomed to destruction, *
happy the one who repays you
   for all you have done to us!

9 Who takes your little ones, *
and dashes them against the rock!

PSALM 138

1 I will give thanks to you, O Lord, with my whole heart; *
before the gods will I sing praise to you.

2 I will bow down towards your holy temple and praise your name,
   because of your love and faithfulness; *
for you have glorified your name
   and your word above all things.

3 In the day that I called to you, you answered me; *
you endued my soul with much strength.

4 All the kings of the earth shall praise you, O Lord, *
for they have heard the words of your mouth.

5 They shall sing of the ways of the Lord, *
that great is the glory of the Lord.

6 Though the Lord be high, he watches over the lowly; *
as for the proud, he perceives them from afar.

7 Though I walk in the midst of trouble,
   you shall preserve me; *
you will stretch forth your hand against the fury of my enemies;
   your right hand shall save me.

8 The Lord shall make good his purpose for me; *
your loving-kindness, O Lord, endures for ever;
   forsake not the work of your hands.

PSALM 139

1   O Lord, you have searched me out and known me; *
    you know my sitting down and my rising up;
        you discern my thoughts from afar.

2   You mark out my journeys and my resting-place *
    and are acquainted with all my ways.

3   For there is not a word on my tongue, *
    but you, O Lord, know it altogether.

4   You keep watch behind and before me *
    and lay your hand upon me.

5   Such knowledge is too wonderful for me; *
    so high that I cannot attain it.

6   Where can I go then from your spirit? *
    or where can I flee from your presence?

7   If I climb up to heaven, you are there; *
    if I make my bed in hell, you are there also.

8   If I take the wings of the morning *
    and dwell in the uttermost parts of the sea,

9   Even there your hand shall lead me, *
    your right hand hold me fast.

10 If I say, 'Surely the darkness will cover me, *
    and the light around me turn to night',

11 Even darkness is not too dark for you;
        the night is as clear as the day; *
    darkness and light to you are both alike.

12 For you yourself created my inmost parts; *
    you knit me together in my mother's womb.

13 I thank you, for I am fearfully and wonderfully made; *
    marvellous are your works, my soul knows well.

14 My frame was not hidden from you, *
when I was made in secret
and woven in the depths of the earth.

15 Your eyes beheld my form, as yet unfinished; *
already in your book were all my members written,

16 As day by day they were fashioned *
when as yet there was none of them.

17 How deep are your counsels to me, O God! *
O how great is the sum of them!

18 If I count them, they are more in number than the sand; *
and at the end, I am still in your presence.

19 O that you would slay the wicked, O God *
that the bloodthirsty might depart from me.

20 They speak against you with wicked intent; *
your enemies take up your name for evil.

21 Do I not oppose those, O Lord, who oppose you? *
do I not abhor those who rise up against you?

22 I am utterly against them; *
they have become my own enemies also.

23 Search me out, O God, and know my heart; *
try me and examine my thoughts.

24 Look well whether there be any way of wickedness in me *
and lead me in the way everlasting.

PSALM 140

1 Deliver me, O Lord, from evildoers; *
and protect me from the violent,

2 Who devise evil in their hearts *
and stir up strife all the day long.

3   They have sharpened their tongues like a serpent; *
adder's poison is under their lips.

4   Keep me, O Lord, from the hands of the wicked; *
protect me from the violent,
    who seek to make me stumble.

5   The proud have laid a snare for me
    and spread out a net of cords; *
they have set traps along my path.

6   I have said to the Lord, 'You are my God; *
listen, O Lord, to the voice of my supplication.

7   'O Lord God, the strength of my salvation, *
you have covered my head in the day of battle.

8   'Do not grant the desires of the wicked, O Lord, *
do not prosper their wicked plans.

9   'Let not those who surround me lift up their heads; *
let the evil of their own lips fall upon them.

10   'Let hot burning coals rain upon them; *
let them be cast into the depths, that they rise not again.'

11   No slanderer shall prosper on the earth, *
and evil shall hunt down the violent to overthrow them.

12   I know that the Lord will bring justice for the oppressed *
and maintain the cause of the needy.

13   Surely, the righteous will give thanks to your name, *
and the upright shall dwell in your presence.

PSALM 141

1   O Lord, I call to you; come to me quickly; *
hear my voice when I cry to you.

2   Let my prayer rise before you as incense, *
the lifting up of my hands as the evening sacrifice.

3   Set a watch before my mouth, O Lord, *
     and guard the door of my lips;

4   Let not my heart incline to any evil thing; *
     let me not be occupied in wickedness with evildoers,
         nor taste the pleasures of their table.

5   Let the righteous smite me in friendly rebuke;
         but let not the oil of the unrighteous anoint my head; *
     for my prayer is continually against their wicked deeds.

6   Let their rulers be overthrown in stony places, *
     that they may know my words are true.

7   As when a plough turns over the earth in furrows, *
     let their bones be scattered at the mouth of the Pit.

8   But my eyes are turned to you, Lord God; *
     in you I take refuge; do not leave me defenceless.

9   Protect me from the snare which they have laid for me *
     and from the traps of the evildoers.

10   Let the wicked fall into their own nets, *
     while I pass by in safety.

PSALM 142

1   I cry to the Lord with my voice; *
     to the Lord I make my supplication.

2   I pour out my complaint before him *
     and tell him of my trouble.

3   When my spirit faints within me, you know my path; *
     in the way wherein I walk have they laid a snare for me.

4   I look to my right hand, and find no one who knows me; *
     I have no place to flee unto, and no one cares for my soul.

5   I cry out to you, O Lord, and say: *
     'You are my refuge, my portion in the land of the living.'

6   Listen to my cry, for I am brought very low; *
     save me from my persecutors, for they are too strong for me.

7   Bring my soul out of prison, that I may give thanks to your name; *
     when you have dealt bountifully with me,
       then shall the righteous gather around me.

PSALM 143

1   Hear my prayer, O Lord,
       and in your faithfulness give ear to my supplications; *
     answer me in your righteousness.

2   Enter not into judgement with your servant, *
     for in your sight shall no one living be justified.

3   For the enemy has pursued me,
       crushing my life to the ground; *
     making me sit in darkness like those long dead.

4   My spirit faints within me; *
     my heart within me is desolate.

5   I remember the time past; I muse upon all your deeds; *
     I consider the works of your hands.

6   I stretch out my hands to you; *
     my soul gasps for you like a thirsty land.

7   O Lord, make haste to answer me; my spirit fails me; *
     hide not your face from me
       lest I be like those who go down to the Pit.

8   Let me hear of your loving-kindness in the morning,
       for in you I put my trust; *
     show me the way that I should walk in,
       for I lift up my soul to you.

9   Deliver me, O Lord, from my enemies, *
     for I flee to you for refuge.

10   Teach me to do what pleases you, for you are my God; *
     let your good spirit lead me on level ground.

11　Revive me, O Lord, for your name's sake; *
　　for your righteousness' sake, bring me out of trouble.

12　In your faithfulness, slay my enemies,
　　　　and destroy all the adversaries of my soul, *
　　for truly I am your servant.

PSALM 144

1　Blessèd be the Lord my rock! *
　　who teaches my hands for war and my fingers for battle;

2　My sure help and my fortress, my castle and my deliverer,
　　　　my shield in whom I trust, *
　　who subdues my people under me.

3　O Lord, what are we that you should consider us? *
　　mere children of earth that you should take thought for us?

4　We are like a breath of wind; *
　　our days pass away like a shadow.

5　Bow your heavens, O Lord, and come down; *
　　touch the mountains and they shall smoke.

6　Cast down your lightning and scatter them; *
　　shoot out your arrows and put them to flight.

7　Reach down your hand from on high; *
　　deliver me and take me out of the great waters,
　　　　from the hand of alien foes,

8　Whose mouth speaks wickedness *
　　and their right hand is the hand of falsehood.

9　O God, I will sing to you a new song; *
　　I will play to you on a ten-stringed harp.

10　You that give salvation to kings *
　　and have delivered David your servant.

11　O save me from the peril of the sword *
　　and deliver me from the hand of alien foes,

12   Whose mouth speaks wickedness *
     and whose right hand is the hand of falsehood;

13   So that our sons in their youth
          may be like well-nurtured plants, *
     and our daughters like pillars
          carved for the corners of the temple;

14   Our barns be filled with all manner of store; *
     our flocks bearing thousands,
          and ten-thousands in our fields;

15   Our cattle be heavy with young; *
     May there be no miscarriage or untimely birth;
          no cry of distress in our streets.

16   Happy are the people whose blessing this is! *
     Happy are the people who have the Lord for their God.

PSALM 145

1   I will exalt you, O God my King, *
     and bless your name for ever and ever.

2   Every day will I bless you *
     and praise your name for ever and ever.

3   Great is the Lord and highly to be praised; *
     his greatness is beyond all searching out.

4   One generation shall praise your works to another *
     and declare your mighty acts.

5   They shall speak of the majesty of your glory; *
     and I will tell of all your wonderful deeds.

6   They shall speak of the might of your marvellous acts, *
     and I will also tell of your greatness.

7   They will pour forth the story of your abundant kindness; *
     and joyfully sing of your righteousness.

8   The Lord is gracious and merciful, *
    long-suffering and of great goodness.

9   The Lord is loving unto everyone *
    and his mercy is over all his creatures.

10 All your works praise you, O Lord, *
    and your faithful servants bless you.

11 They tell of the glory of your kingdom *
    and speak of your mighty power;

12 To make known to all peoples your mighty acts *
    and the glorious splendour of your kingdom.

13 Your kingdom is an everlasting kingdom; *
    your dominion endures throughout all ages.

14 The Lord is sure in all his words *
    and faithful in all his deeds.

15 The Lord upholds all those who fall; *
    and lifts up all those who are bowed down.

16 The eyes of all wait upon you, O Lord, *
    and you give them their food in due season.

17 You open wide your hand *
    and fill all things living with plenty.

18 The Lord is righteous in all his ways *
    and loving in all his works.

19 The Lord is near to those who call upon him, *
    to all who call upon him faithfully.

20 He fulfils the desire of those who fear him, *
    he hears their cry and saves them.

21 The Lord watches over those who love him, *
    but all the wicked shall he destroy.

22 My mouth shall speak the praise of the Lord, *
    and let all flesh bless his holy name for ever and ever.

PSALM 146

1   Alleluia!
      Praise the Lord, O my soul!
      While I live will I praise the Lord; *
    as long as I have any being,
      I will sing praises to my God.

2   Put not your trust in princes,
      nor in any child of earth, *
    for there is no help in them.

3   When their breath goes out, they return to the earth; *
    on that day all their thoughts perish.

4   Happy are they that have the God of Jacob for their help! *
    whose hope is set on the Lord their God;

5   Who made heaven and earth,
      the sea and all that is in them; *
    who keeps his promise for ever;

6   Who gives justice to those that suffer wrong, *
    and bread to those who hunger.

7   The Lord looses those that are bound; *
    the Lord opens the eyes of the blind;

8   The Lord lifts up those who are bowed down; *
    the Lord loves the righteous;

9   The Lord watches over the stranger in the land;
      he upholds the orphan and widow; *
    but the way of the wicked he turns upside down.

10   The Lord shall reign for ever, *
    your God, O Zion, throughout all generations.
      Alleluia!

PSALM 147

1   Alleluia!
       How good it is to make music for our God! *
    How joyful to honour him with praise!

2   The Lord builds up Jerusalem; *
    and gathers together the outcasts of Israel.

3   He heals the brokenhearted *
    and binds up all their wounds.

4   He counts the number of the stars *
    and calls them all by their names.

5   Great is our Lord and mighty in power; *
    his wisdom is beyond all telling.

6   The Lord lifts up the poor, *
    but casts down the wicked to the ground.

7   Sing to the Lord with thanksgiving; *
    make music to our God upon the lyre;

8   Who covers the heavens with clouds *
    and prepares rain for the earth;

9   Who makes grass to grow upon the mountains *
    and green plants to serve our needs.

10 He gives the beasts their food *
    and the young ravens when they cry.

11 He has no desire for the strength of a war-horse, *
    no need of the soldier's strong legs;

12 But the Lord delights in those who fear him, *
    who put their trust in his steadfast love.

13 Sing praise to the Lord, O Jerusalem; *
    praise your God, O Zion;

14   For he has strengthened the bars of your gates *
     and has blessed your children within you.

15   He has established peace in your borders; *
     and satisfies you with the finest wheat.

16   He sends forth his command to the earth, *
     and his word runs very swiftly.

17   He gives snow like wool, *
     and scatters the hoarfrost like ashes.

18   He casts down his hailstones like morsels of bread; *
     who can endure his frost?

19   He sends forth his word and melts them; *
     he blows with his wind and the waters flow.

20   He declares his word to Jacob, *
     his statutes and judgements to Israel.

21   He has not dealt so with any other nation; *
     they do not know his laws.
     Alleluia!

PSALM 148

1   Alleluia!
     Praise the Lord from the heavens; *
  praise him in the heights.

2   Praise him, all you angels of his; *
     praise him, all his host.

3   Praise him, sun and moon; *
     praise him, all you stars of light.

4   Praise him, heaven of heavens, *
     and you waters above the heavens.

5   Let them praise the name of the Lord; *
     for he commanded and they were created.

6   He made them fast for ever and ever; *
      he gave them a law which shall not pass away.

7   Praise the Lord from the earth, *
      you sea-monsters and all deeps;

8   Fire and hail, snow and mist, *
      tempestuous wind, fulfilling his word;

9   Mountains and all hills, *
      fruitful trees and all cedars;

10   Wild beasts and all cattle, *
      creeping things and birds on the wing;

11   Kings of the earth and all peoples, *
      princes and all rulers of the world;

12   Young men and maidens,
      the old and children together; *
    let them praise the name of the Lord.

13   For his name only is exalted, *
      his splendour above earth and heaven.

14   He has raised up the horn of his people
      and praise for all his faithful servants, *
    the children of Israel, a people who are near him.
      Alleluia!

PSALM 149

1   Alleluia!
      O sing to the Lord a new song; *
    his praise in the congregation of the faithful.

2   Let Israel rejoice in its maker; *
      let the children of Zion be joyful in their king.

3   Let them praise his name in the dance; *
      let them sing praise to him with timbrel and lyre.

4   For the Lord has pleasure in his people *
     and adorns the poor with salvation.

5   Let the faithful be joyful in glory; *
     let them rejoice in their ranks;

6   With the praises of God in their throat *
     and a two-edged sword in their hand;

7   To execute vengeance on the nations *
     and punishment on the peoples;

8   To bind their kings in chains *
     and their nobles with links of iron;

9   To execute on them the judgement decreed; *
     such honour have all his faithful servants.
        Alleluia!

PSALM 150

1   Alleluia!
        O praise God in his holiness; *
     praise him in the firmament of his power.

2   Praise him for his mighty acts; *
     praise him for the greatness of his strength.

3   Praise him with the blast of the trumpet; *
     praise him upon the harp and lyre.

4   Praise him with timbrel and dances; *
     praise him upon the strings and pipe.

5   Praise him with ringing cymbals; *
     praise him upon the clashing cymbals.

6   Let everything that has breath *
     praise the Lord.
        Alleluia!

Notes

The Hebrew text of the psalms poses a range of complex issues for those who have to provide a text of the psalms in English suitable for liturgical use. The highly selective notes below are given as illustrations of some of the major general issues which those who have prepared *The Psalter 1998* have had to face. These notes are not intended to be comprehensive, nor definitive, and should not be treated as such.

1   *Ben adam* – son of man

a)   In the original Hebrew, the word translated as 'man' in Psalm 8.4a is generic (i.e. inclusive of men and women), and 'son of man' in 4b is written in poetic parallel with the same sense as 4a (this feature, sometimes known as 'synonymous parallelism' is a characteristic of Hebrew poetry). The alternative version of verses 4-6 (*The Psalter 1998* page 10) seeks to bring out this parallelism. But the passage is quoted at Hebrews 2.6-8 with reference to Jesus, and 'son of man' is the term by which Jesus referred to himself. Preserving the link with Jesus has been taken to outweigh the desire for inclusive language in the main text of Psalm 8 in *The Psalter 1998*.

b)   At Psalm 80.18 the phrase *ben adam* is not generic. It referred originally to the king and later to the Messiah, so there is the same case as that outlined above for retaining 'son of man' in English. Psalm 144.3 is very similar to Psalm 8.4, but here the reference is clearly generic and not messianic.

2   *Elohim*

a)   In Psalm 8.5 the rendering of the Septuagint and Hebrews 2.7 is 'little lower than the angels'. The Hebrew word rendered as 'angels' is *elohim*, which can mean God or gods – lesser divine or supernatural beings, sometimes referring to human authorities (cf. Psalm 82.1,6, quoted at John 10.34).

b)   The meaning of the word *elohim* at Psalm 45.6 (a psalm addressed to the king) is ambiguous. It can be translated, 'Your throne, O God, endures for ever', with *elohim* used for a human authority (see Note 2a), or 'Your throne is the throne of God; it endures for ever'. It is quoted at Hebrews 1.8, which is itself also ambiguous: either, 'Your throne, O God, endures for ever' or, less probably, 'God is your throne for ever'. In both places those who have prepared *The Psalter 1998* have opted on balance to use English phraseology which is allowed by the Hebrew and which also reflects a developed understanding of the divinity of Christ.

3   Singular and plural personal pronouns

In Psalm 69.28b (27 in the Hebrew) one Hebrew manuscript and the Syriac read, 'him whom you have pierced', but the rest of the Hebrew manuscripts and the Septuagint read, 'those whom . . .'. Psalm 69.28a could be either singular or plural – the Septuagint has the singular. Since the New Testament writers read this psalm messianically in the light of Christ's passion, the singular has been retained in both places in *The Psalter 1998*.

4   Places where New Testament writers quote the Old Testament in a version different from the Hebrew:

a)   In Hebrew Amos 9.12 reads, 'in order that they may possess the remnant of Edom, and all the nations who are called by my name'. At Acts 15.17 James says, in line with the Septuagint, 'in order that the remnant of men may seek the Lord, and all the nations upon whom my name has been called'. 'Edom' and 'men' (*adam*) share the same consonants; 'possess' has become 'seek' by the change of one consonant.

b)   At Ephesians 4.8 Paul, like the Targum (the Jewish liturgical paraphrase of the Hebrew text), quotes Psalm 68.18 as 'he gave gifts to men', instead of 'he received gifts from men'.

c)   New Testament writers sometimes adapted and reapplied Old Testament texts. For example, at Hebrews 1.10 the word 'Lord' (Greek *kurios*) is inserted in Psalm 102.25 (Psalm 101.26 in Greek), exploiting the use of *kurios* both as a title for God and for earthly lords, (cf. Psalm 110.1). As a result, the Hebrews passage then becomes a dialogue between God and the Messiah.

5   Important and recurring words in the psalms which can be translated in different ways according to context and in the light of the developing tradition:

a)   *Hesedh* means 'goodness, kindness', with a nuance of fidelity. It usually refers to God, and is rendered 'steadfast love', 'faithful love', 'loving-kindness', or (following the Coverdale Psalter in *The Book of Common Prayer 1662*) 'mercy', as in the refrain 'for his mercy endures for ever' (Psalm 136).

b) *Hasidh*, an adjective used as a noun, means 'pious, godly', and is usually rendered 'faithful (one)', as at Psalm 16.10, where Coverdale followed the Septuagint's 'holy one', quoted in Acts 2.27.

c) *Emeth*, 'truth' (cognate with *Amen*), has the basic meaning of 'sureness, reliability', and is sometimes better translated 'faithfulness', as at Psalm 54.5.

d) *Tsedekh*, traditionally translated 'righteousness', means being or acting in accord with what is right; in God's case this could mean giving victory or vindication. In Psalm 4.1 'God of my righteousness' meant originally 'God who maintains my cause'; in Psalm 4.5 'sacrifice of righteousness' could be 'correct sacrifice', and in Psalm 23.3 'paths of righteousness' could be 'right paths'. But usually 'righteousness' has been retained since it can cover these and other important meanings; for example, sacrifice consisting of or springing from right attitude or conduct, alongside right (animal) sacrifices, as at Psalm 51.20.

e) *Yeshua*, traditionally 'salvation', has a this-worldly sense of deliverance or victory, but 'salvation' has usually been retained as allowing for a wider meaning.

f) *Nephesh*, 'soul', similarly can have a concrete meaning, 'neck or throat' ('his neck was ringed with iron', rather than 'the iron entered into his soul' at Psalm 105.18). It usually refers to the whole person and can be rendered by 'life' or simply by the personal pronoun. There is no body/soul distinction in the Hebrew, but Coverdale's 'soul' has often been retained (as at Psalm 49.8,16), as maintaining a wider dimension of meaning than the alternatives.

g) *Sheol*, traditionally 'hell', is simply, like the Greek Hades, the underworld, the place of the dead. It is usually rendered 'the Pit', or 'the grave', or 'the land of death', but at Psalm 139.7 the context perhaps justifies retaining 'hell'.

h) *Adam* or *enosh*, meaning 'man' generically, often in the phrase 'son of man', poses problems for the use of inclusive language in English. The link of *adam* with *adamah*, earth (Genesis 2.7) makes 'child of earth' often an appropriate rendering, as at Psalm 146.2,3. 'Mortals' is not always satisfactory and 'humans' makes poor poetry. 'Son of man' has been retained at Psalms 8.4 and 80.18 because of New Testament resonances (see Note 1a).

NB *Psalm references in these Notes are to* The Psalter 1998. *The verse numbers in other translations and in the Hebrew and Greek may differ slightly.*

Music Appendix

Contents

Introduction

The Music Appendix to *The Psalter 1998* has been prepared by the Liturgical Publishing Group acting on the advice of its Music Reference Group.

The musical settings which follow are offered as examples of the ways in which these psalms can be sung – they are in no sense definitive. The settings are in a mixture of styles, old and new, and designed for a variety of uses – for example:

- for unaccompanied singing;
- for cantor-led worship;
- for use with instruments;
- for use with Taizé-style repeated chants;
- for full involvement of SATB choir (with descant), organist and congregation.

Where there are refrains, they vary in style and mood: meditative, joyous, reflective and peaceful. Many of the settings are designed for unaccompanied voices, rather than being reliant on keyboard accompaniment.

Different styles of pointing are given, including the most common pointing for use with plainchant and Anglican chant. The under-lining which indicates the move from reciting note is now a well-established technique giving non-specialists the opportunity to sing psalms well. The use of note shapes beneath or above the text gives extra help in matching notes to syllables. Psalms 4, 91 and 134 are grouped together at the end of the Appendix and pointed for plainchant, the common form for those familiar with using these psalms for Compline.

The *gloria patri* is included for use at Morning and Evening Prayer. It should be omitted at the Eucharist.

The aim of this approach is to stimulate ideas as to how psalms can be sung – everywhere from cathedrals and large churches to smaller congregations with few musical resources. We hope that there is something here for everyone. The settings could form a resource for those running workshops or training days for parish music leaders or congregations. The variety also reflects the need to match the style of music to the text of the psalm – for example, the celebration of Psalm 150 is expressed in joyous music, whereas Psalms 42 and 43 are set in a more meditative style.

We hope that the arrival of the new *Common Worship* liturgies will stimulate the singing of psalms and we would welcome your views on the various approaches demonstrated in this Appendix. They may raise questions rather than provide answers: should psalms for the Eucharist and the office differ in style? Should musical style relate to a particular community or to particular psalms? Are refrains an aid to participation in psalmody or do they inhibit particapation? A questionnaire has been provided for this purpose and we hope to hear from as many people as possible – members of congregations, cantors, choir members, organists or instrumentalists – who seek to offer worship to God as they sing the ancient songs of his people.

+John Guildford
Chairman
General Synod Liturgical Publishing Group

N.B. The musicians setting these psalms were working on an earlier version of the psalter text. Minor changes have since been made by the Psalter Group, particularly to Psalms 4, 42 and 100, as part of the continuing process of revision which will carry on during 1999 following responses from this edition.

PSALM 4

Robert Fielding

1 Answer me, O God of my righteousness, <u>as</u> I call to you;*
   you set me at liberty when I was hard-pressed;
      have mercy on me and <u>hear</u> my prayer.

2 How long will you people dis-<u>honour</u> my glory;*
   how long will you love vain things and <u>seek</u> af-ter falsehood?

3 But know that the Lord has chosen to himself the <u>one that</u> is faithful;*
   when I call upon the Lord, <u>he</u> will hear me.

4 Stand in <u>awe</u>, and sin not;*
   commune with your own heart upon your bed, <u>and</u> be still.

5 Offer the <u>sacrifices</u> of righteousness*
   and put your trust <u>in</u> the Lord.

6 There are many that say, Who will show us <u>an</u>-y good?*
   Lift up the light of your countenance up<u>on us</u>, O Lord.

7 You will put gladness <u>in</u> my heart,*
   more than when their corn and wine and <u>oil</u> increase.

8 I will lie down and <u>sleep</u> in peace;*
   for it is you, Lord, only, who make me <u>dwell</u> in safety.

   Glory to the Father and <u>to</u> the Son*
      and to the <u>Ho</u>-ly Spirit;
   as it was in the be-<u>ginning</u> is now*
      and shall be for <u>ever</u>. Amen.

PSALM 4

Alan Harwood

Refrain

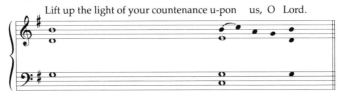

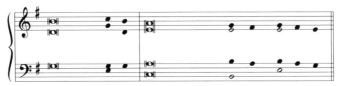

1   Answer me, O God of my righteousness, as I call to you;*
    you set me at liberty when I was hard-pressed;
      have mercy on me and hear my prayer.

2   How long will you people dishonour my glory;*
    how long will you love vain things and seek af-ter falsehood?

3   But know that the Lord has chosen to himself the one that is faith-ful;*
    when I call upon the Lord, he will hear me.

4   Stand in awe, and sin not;*
    commune with your own heart upon your bed, and be still.

5   Offer the sacrifices of right-eousness*
    and put your trust in the Lord.

6   There are many that say, Who will show us an-y good?*
    Lift up the light of your countenance upon us, O Lord.

7   You will put gladness in my heart,*
    more than when their corn and wine and oil increase.

8   I will lie down and sleep in peace;*
    for it is you, Lord, only, who make me dwell in safety.

    Glory to the Father and to the Son*
      and to the Ho-ly Spirit;
    as it was in the beginning is now*
      and shall be for ev-er. Amen.

PSALM 4

K. J. Pye

1 Answer me, O God of my righteousness, / as I / call to you;*
    you set me at liberty when I was hard-pressed;
        have / mercy on me • and / hear my / prayer.

2 How long will you people dis-/ honour • my / glory;*
    how long will you love / vain things • and / seek aft - er / falsehood?

3 But know that the Lord has chosen to himself the / one that • is / faithful;*
    when I call upon the / Lo - rd, / he will / hear me.

4 Stand in / awe, and / sin not;*
    commune with your own / heart up - on your / bed, and • be / still.

5 Offer the / sacrifices • of / righteousness*
    and / put your / trust in • the / Lord.

6 There are many that say, Who will / show us • any / good?*
    Lift up the light of your / countenance • up-/ on us, • O / Lord.

7 You will put / gladness • in my / heart,*
    more than when their corn and / wine and / oil in-/ crease.

8 I will lie down and / sleep in / peace;*
    for it is you, Lord, only, who / make me / dwell in / safety.

    Glory to the Father and / to the / Son*
      and / to the / Ho-ly / Spirit;
    as it was in the be-/ ginning • is / now*
      and shall be for / ev-er. / A-/ men.

PSALM 23

Robert Fielding

Refrain

I will dwell in the house___ of the Lord___ for ev- er, for he___ shall___ re-fresh my soul.

Flowing with movement

Tone

Refrain and Tone may use optional
unison melody, SATB or keyboard
accompaniment.

1 The Lord is my shepherd;*
  therefore can I lack nothing.

2 He makes me lie down in green pastures*
  and leads me beside still waters. **[R]**

3 He shall refresh my soul*
  and guide me in the paths of righteousness for his name's sake.

4 Even though I walk through the valley of the shadow of death,
    I will fear no evil;*
  for you are with me;
    your rod and your staff, they comfort me. **[R]**

5 You have spread a table before me
    in the presence of those who trouble me;*
  you have anointed my head with oil
    and my cup shall be full.

6 Surely, goodness and loving-mercy shall follow me
    all the days of my life*
  and I will dwell in the house of the Lord for ever.

  Glory to the Father and to the Son*
    and to the Ho-ly Spirit;
  as it was in the beginning is now*
    and shall be for ever. Amen. **[R]**

PSALM 23

Peter Moger

Refrain

1. The Lord / is my / shepherd;*
   therefore / can I • lack / nothing.

2. He makes me lie down in / green / pastures*
   and leads me be- / side still / waters.　　　　　　　　　　**[R]**

3. He shall re- / fresh my / soul*
   and guide me in the paths of / righteousness • for his / name's sake.

4. Even though I walk through the valley of the shadow of death,
   　I will / fear no / evil;*
   for you are with me;
   　your rod and your / staff, they / comfort me.　　　　　**[R]**

5. You have spread a table before me
   　in the presence of / those who / trouble me;*
   you have anointed my head with oil
   　and my / cup shall • be / full.

6. Surely, goodness and loving-mercy shall follow me
   　all the / days of • my / life*
   and I will dwell in the house of the / Lord for / ever.　　**[R]**

   Glory to the Father / and to • the / Son*
   　and to the / Ho-ly / Spirit;
   as it was in the be-/ ginning • is / now*
   　and shall be for / ev-er. A-/ men.　　　　　　　　　　**[R]**

PSALM 42

Sister Agnes Mary SPB

Refrain

Why are you so full of heaviness, O my soul? O put your trust in God.

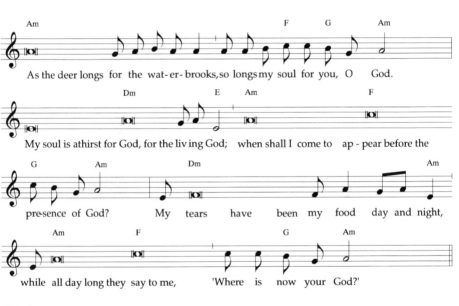

As the deer longs for the wat-er-brooks, so longs my soul for you, O God.

My soul is athirst for God, for the liv ing God; when shall I come to ap - pear before the

pre-sence of God? My tears have been my food day and night,

while all day long they say to me, 'Where is now your God?'

Refrain

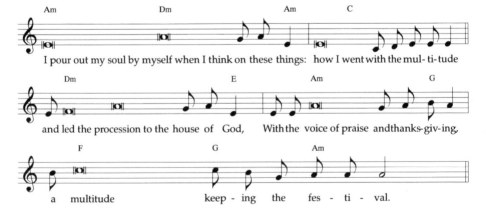

I pour out my soul by myself when I think on these things: how I went with the mul-ti-tude

and led the procession to the house of God, With the voice of praise and thanks-giv-ing,

a multitude keep-ing the fes-ti-val.

216

Why are you so full of heaviness, O my soul? and why are you so disquie-ted with-in me?

O put your trust in God; for I will yet give him thanks,

who is the help of my countenance, and my God.

Refrain

My soul is hea - vy with - in me; there-fore I will re - mem-ber you

from the source of the Jor - dan, and from Hermon and the hill of Mi- zar.

Deep calls to deep in the roar of your wa - ter - falls;

all your waves and your floods have gone o - ver me.

Refrain

The Lord will grant his loving-kindness in the day-time; in the night his song is with me,

a prayer to the God of my life. I will say to God my rock,

'Why have you for-got-ten me? and why go I so heavily while the en-e-my oppresses me?'

As though they would crush my very bones, my en - e - mies mock me;

while they say to me all the day long, 'Where now is your God?'

Why are you so full of heaviness, O my soul? and why are you so disqui-e-ted with-in me?

O put your trust in God; for I will yet give him thanks,

who is the help of my countenance, and my God.

Refrain

PSALM 43

Give judgement for me, O God, and defend my cause against an un-god-ly peo-ple;

O de-liver me from the de-ceit-ful and the wick ed. For you are the God of my re-fuge;

why have you cast me from you? and why go I so heavily while the e-ne-my op-presses me?

Refrain

O send out your light and your truth, that they may lead me,
and bring me to your holy hill and to your dwell-ing; That I may go to the al-tar of God,
to the God of my joy and glad-ness; and on the harp will I give thanks to you,
O God my God.

Why are you so full of heaviness, O my soul? and why are you so disqui-e-ted with-in me?

O put your trust in God; for I will yet give him thanks,
who is the help of my countenance, and my God.

Refrain

Glory to the Father and to the Son, and to the Ho - ly Spi - rit;
as it was in the be-gin-ning is now, and shall be for ev - er. A - men.

Refrain

PSALMS 42 – 43

Originally constituting one song of lament, Psalms 42 and 43 have here been set together by Sister Agnes Mary SPB.

The refrain 'Why are you so full of heaviness', encloses three strophes, the third of which begins Psalm 43. This, and the fact that psalm 42 carried a title and 43 dis not, gives strength to the use of psalm 43 as a continuation of 42.

In many lectionaries, the two psalms appear both together and separately. Three further settings of Psalm 43 alone are given for optional use.

Notes for Psalms 42–43

This setting should be sung with a free rhythm, giving expression to the words.

Ideally, it would have a harp-like accompaniment with broken chords. However, it could be accompanied by sustained chords on an organ. It could also be sung unaccompanied.

The four-part setting of the refrain is optional. It can equally well be sung with the melody line only.

If Psalm 43 is sung alone, it should begin with the refrain.

Sister Agnes Mary SPB

PSALM 43

Verses (Choir)

Freely chanted, with or without accompaniment.

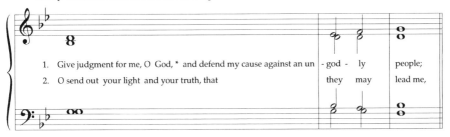

1. Give judgment for me, O God, * and defend my cause against an un-god-ly people;
2. O send out your light and your truth, that they may lead me,

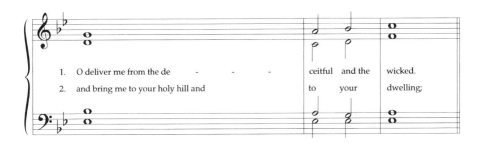

1. O deliver me from the de - - - ceitful and the wicked.
2. and bring me to your holy hill and to your dwelling;

crescendo

1. For you are the God of my refuge; * why have you cast me from you?
2. That I may go to the altar of God, * to the God of my joy and gladness;

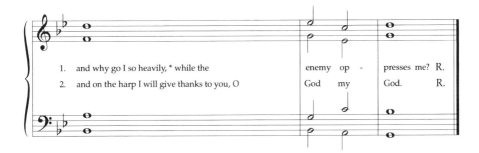

1. and why go I so heavily, * while the enemy op - presses me? R.
2. and on the harp I will give thanks to you, O God my God. R.

PSALM 43

Geoff Weaver

2. you are the God of my re-fuge; _____ why have you cast _____ me from you? and why go I so hea-vi-ly, _____ while the e-ne-my _____ opp-ress-es me? 3. send out your light and your truth, that they _____ may lead me, and bring me _____ to your

ho - ly hill,_____ to your ho - ly hill _____

and to your dwel - ling; _____ 4. That I may go to the

al - tar of God, to the God of my joy and glad - ness;

and on the harp will I give thanks to you, _____ O

God my God.

Refrain

Why are you so full of hea-vi-ness, O my soul? and why are you so dis-qui-e-ted with-in me? O put your trust in God; for I will yet give him

thanks, who is the help of my coun - te - nance,_____ and my God._____ Glo - ry to _____ the Fa - ther _____ and to _____ the Son _____ and to the Ho - ly Spi - rit;_____

as it was ___ in the be-gin-ning is now and shall be for -

e - ver. ___ A - men. ___ *poco rit.* A -

men. ___ *poco rit.*

PSALM 43

Jonathan Priestland Young

Refrain

Why are you so full of hea-vi-ness, O my soul? O put your trust ___ in God.

Verses

Begin stanzas 1 & 2 here · Begin stanza 3 here

1. Give judgement for *me*, O God, and defend my cause against an un - *god - ly* people;
2. O send out your light *and* *your* truth that *they may* lead me
3. Why are you so full of heaviness, O *my* soul?

Begin *Gloria Patri* here

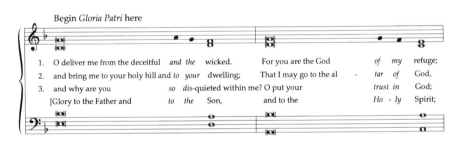

1. O deliver me from the deceitful *and the* wicked. For you are the God *of* *my* refuge;
2. and bring me to your holy hill and *to* *your* dwelling; That I may go to the al - *tar* *of* God,
3. and why are you *so* *dis*-quieted within me? O put your *trust in* God;
   [Glory to the Father and *to* *the* Son, and to the *Ho* - *ly* Spirit;

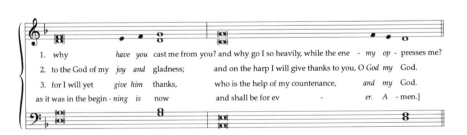

1. why *have* *you* cast me from you? and why go I so heavily, while the ene - *my* op - presses me?
2. to the God of my *joy* *and* gladness; and on the harp I will give thanks to you, O *God* *my* God.
3. for I will yet *give* *him* thanks, who is the help of my countenance, *and* *my* God.
   as it was in the begin - *ning* *is* now and shall be for ev - *er*. A - men.]

PSALM 91

Br. Reginald SSF

Refrain

You, O Lord, are my re - fuge. my God in whom I put my trust.

Tone

1 Whoever dwells in the shelter of the Most High,*
    and abides under the shadow of the Almighty,

2 Shall say to the Lord, 'My refuge and my stronghold,*
    my God in whom I put my trust'.

3 For he shall deliver you from the snare of the fowler*
    and from the deadly curse.

4 He shall cover you with his wings,
        and you shall be safe under his feathers;*
    his faithfulness shall be your shield and buckler.   [R]

5 You shall not be afraid of any terror by night,*
    nor the arrow that flies by day;

6 Of the pestilence that stalks in darkness,*
    nor of the sickness that destroys at noonday.

7 Though a thousand fall at your side
   and ten thousand at your right hand,*
   yet it shall not come near you.

8 Your eyes have only to behold*
   to see the reward of the wicked.   [R]

9 Because you have made the Lord your refuge,*
   and the Most High your stronghold,

10 There shall no evil happen to you,*
   neither shall any plague come near your tent.

11 For he shall give his angels charge over you,*
   to keep you in all your ways.

12 They shall bear you in their hands,*
   lest you dash your foot against a stone.   [R]

13 You shall tread upon the dragon and adder;*
   the lion and the serpent you shall trample under your feet.

14 Because you have set your love upon me,
   therefore will I deliver you;*
   I will lift you up, because you know my name.

15 You will call upon me and I will answer you;*
   I am with you in trouble,
   I will deliver you and bring you to honour.

16 With long life will I satisfy you;*
   and show you my salvation.

   Glory to the Father and to the Son*
   and to the Holy Spirit;
   as it was in the beginning is now*
   and shall be for ever. Amen.   [R]

PSALM 100

Rosemary Field

1 O be joyful in the Lord, all the earth;*
   serve the Lord with gladness
      and come before his presence with a song.

2 Know that the Lord is God;*
   it is he that has made us and we are his;
      we are his people and the sheep of his pasture.   **[R]**

3 Enter his gates with thanksgiving,
      and his courts with praise;*
   give thanks to him and bless his name.

4 For the Lord is gracious; his love is ever - lasting;*
   and his faithfulness endures from generation to ge - ne - ration. **[R]**

   Glory to the Father and to the Son*
      and to the Ho - ly Spirit;
   as it was in the beginning is now*
      and shall be for ever. A - men.   **[R]**

PSALM 100

Geoff Weaver

Refrain

En-ter his gates with thanks-gi-ving, and his courts with shouts of praise.

2 Know that the Lord is God; it is he that has made us and we are his; we are his peo-ple and the sheep of his pas-ture.

Ease tempo a little

Tempo come prima

Refrain

En - ter his gates with thanks - gi - ving, and his courts with shouts of praise. 4 For the Lord is gra - cious; his love is e - ver - last - ing; and his faith - ful - ness en - dures from gen - e - ra - tion to gen - e - ra - tion.

Ease tempo a little

gin - ning is now _____ and shall be for e - ver. _____ A -

men. _____ A - men. _____ A - men. _____

PSALM 100

Refrain

Con brio

Geoff Weaver

En - ter his gates with thanks-gi - ving, _____ and his

courts _____ with shouts _____ of praise. _____

PSALM 134

John Harper

Refrain

Tone

1 Come <u>bless</u> the Lord,
    all you <u>ser</u>-vants <u>of</u> the Lord,
    you <u>that</u> by night stand <u>in</u> the <u>house of</u> the Lord   **[R]**

2 Lift up your hands toward the <u>ho</u>-ly presence
    [- -] and <u>bless</u> the Lord.

3 The Lord who made <u>heaven</u> and earth
    give you <u>bless</u>-ing <u>out</u> of Zion.   **[R]**

    Glory to the Father and <u>to</u> the Son
      and <u>to</u> the <u>Ho</u>-ly Spirit;
    as it was in the be<u>ginn</u>ing is now
      and shall <u>be</u> for <u>ever</u>. Amen.   **[R]**

Underlined words or syllables are sung to the black notes of the tone.
The second half of verse 2 begins on the third note of the tone (2nd half).

PSALM 134

Peter Moger

PSALM 134

The Simple Ostinato part could be played on a variety of instruments.
The Melody 1 in C part was conceived as a violin part and the Melody 2 in C as a flute part,
but the choice for both may be flexible. The B♭ part is really intended for trumpet and should
be used sparingly.

Peter Moger

PSALM 150

the Lord.____ **Al - le - lu - ia,** **al - le - lu - ia!**____

Glo - ry____ to the Fath - er and to the Son and to the Ho - ly

Spi - rit;____ **al - le - lu - ia,** ____ **al - le - lu - ia;** ____ as it was in the be -

gin - ning is now and shall be for e - ver.____ A - men,

a - men.____ **A - men,** **a - men,** Al - le -

lu - ia, ____ al - le - lu - ia, ____ **Al - le - lu - ia,** ____ **al - le - lu - ia!** ____

This setting is a dialogue between choir/cantor and people. There is no accompaniment; clapping or percussion will maintain the pulse and there is ample opportunity for vocalists or instrumentalists to embellish or improvize around the melody.

PSALM 4

Cum invocarem

1 Answer me, O God of my righteousness, as I *call* to‿you;*
 you set me at liberty when I was hard-pressed;
  have mercy on *me* and hear my‿prayer.

2 How long will you people dishonour my *glo*-ry;*
 how long will you love vain things and seek *af*-ter falsehood?

3 But know that the Lord has chosen to himself the one that is *faith*-ful;*
 when I call upon the Lord, *he* will hear me.

4 Stand in awe, and *sin* not;*
 commune with your own heart upon your *bed*, and be still.

5 Offer the sacrifices of *right*-eous‿ness*
 and put your *trust* in the Lord.

6 There are many that say, Who will show us any *good*?*
 Lift up the light of your countenance u-*pon* us, O Lord.

7 You will put gladness in my *heart*,*
 more than when their corn and *wine* and oil in‿crease.

8 I will lie down and sleep in *peace*;*
 for it is you, Lord, only, who make me *dwell* in safety.

 Glory to the Father and to the *Son**
  and to the *Ho*-ly Spirit;
 as it was in the beginning is *now**
  and shall be for *ev*-er. Amen.

The opening two notes of this psalm tone are used in verse 1 only (*Ans-wer*).

Italicized syllables are sung to the note following reciting notes (♮).

The final note in bar 1 of the tone is not always used (vv. 6, 7, 8 and *Gloria Patri*).

The sign‿is used when two words or syllables are both sung to the last note of the tone.

PSALM 91

Qui habitat

1 Whoever dwells in the shelter of the Most *High*,*
and abides under the shadow of *the* Almighty,

2 Shall say to the Lord, 'My refuge and my *strong*-hold,*
my God in *whom* I put my trust'.

3 For he shall deliver you from the snare of the *fow*-ler*
and *from* the dea-dly curse.

4 He shall cover you with his wings,
and you shall be safe under his *fea*-thers;*
his faithfulness shall be your *shield* and buckler.

5 You shall not be afraid of any terror by *night*,*
nor the arrow that *flïes* by day;

6 Of the pestilence that stalks in *dark*-ness,*
nor of the sickness that de-*stroys* at noonday.

7 Though a thousand fall at your side
and ten thousand at your right *hand*,*
yet it shall *not* come near you.

8 Your eyes have only to be-*hold**
to see the reward *of* the wicked.

9 Because you have made the Lord your *re*-fuge,*
and the Most *High* your stronghold,

10 There shall no evil happen to *you*,*
neither shall any *plague* come near your tent.

11 For he shall give his angels charge over *you*,*
   to keep *you* in all your ⁀ways.

12 They shall bear you in their *hands*,*
   lest you dash your *foot* against a ⁀stone.

13 You shall tread upon the dragon and *ad*-der;*
   the lion and the serpent you shall trample *un*-der your feet.

14 Because you have set your love upon me,
      therefore will I de-*li*-ver ⁀you;*
   I will lift you up, be-*cause* you know my ⁀name.

15 You will call upon me and I will *ans*-wer ⁀you;*
   I am with you in trouble,
      I will deliver you and bring *you* to honour.

16 With long life will I satisfy *you*;*
   and show you *my* salvation.

   Glory to the Father and to the *Son**
      and to the *Ho*-ly Spirit;
   as it was in the beginning is *now**
      and shall be for *ev*-er. Amen.

The opening two notes of this psalm tone are used in verse 1 only (*Who ev*...).

Italicized syllables are sung to the note following reciting notes (♮).

The final note in bar 1 of the tone is not always used (vv. 1, 5, 7 etc. and *Gloria Patri*).

The sign⁀ is used when two words or syllables are both sung to the last note of the tone.

The two dots over *ë* in the word *fliës* in verse 5 indicate two notes to be sung to one syllable.

PSALM 134

Ecce nunc

1 Come, bless the Lord,
    all you servants of the *Lord*,*
    you that by night stand in the *house* of the Lord.

2 Lift up your hands towards the holy *pre*-sence*
    and *blëss* the Lord.

3 The Lord who made heaven and *earth**
    give you blessing *out* of Zion.

   Glory to the Father and to the *Son**
    and to the *Ho*-ly Spirit;
   as it was in the beginning is *now**
    and shall be for *ev*-er. Amen.

The opening two notes of this psalm tone are used in verse 1 only (*Come, bless*).

Italicized syllables are sung to the note following reciting notes (♮).

Only verse 2 makes use of the small note at the end of bar 1 for the syllable '-sence'.

The two dots over the word *blëss* in verse 2 indicate two notes to be sung to one syllable.

Questionnaire

Questionnaire

We would welcome comment from any users of this book, so that these may be taken into account as further work is done on the draft psalter. Please copy this questionnaire (enlarging it to A4 size, if possible), and, when you have completed it, send it as soon as possible, preferably before 15 June 1999, to: The Secretary to the Liturgical Commission, **Re Psalter Survey**, General Synod Office, Church House, Great Smith Street, LONDON, SW1P 3NZ.

Style of English

1 (a) Do you think that a rich and vivid picture of God's activity, suitable for use in worship, emerges from *The Psalter 1998*?

Yes ☐   No ☐

(b) Do you find the use of inclusive language with respect to people in *The Psalter 1998* helpful?

Yes ☐   No ☐

Please state your reason(s):

(c) In which kinds of services do you usually use the psalms? Please tick as many categories as apply.

Traditional language (e.g. BCP; ASB Rite B)

Eucharistic ☐

Morning Prayer ☐

Evening Prayer/Evensong ☐

Other (please state) ☐

Contemporary language (e.g. ASB Rite A)

Eucharistic ☐

Morning Prayer ☐

Evening Prayer/Evensong ☐

'Family' service ☐

Other (please state) ☐

(d) Do you consider that the quality of the language in *The Psalter 1998* would be suitable for corporate recitation at those services?

Yes ☐   No ☐

Please state your reason(s):

(e) Overall is *The Psalter 1998* suitable for use at services which you attend?

Yes ☐   No ☐

Please state your reason(s):

Layout

2 (a) In what ways, if any, could the layout of the text of the psalms be improved?

(b) Is it helpful to have an asterisk * marking the half-way point in each verse of the psalms?

Yes ☐   No ☐

Please suggest any ways in which this system could be improved:

(c) Would you find the inclusion of brackets around difficult verses of the psalms, as used in the ASB Psalter, helpful for worship?

Yes ☐ No ☐

Music

3 (a) Is it helpful to have musical examples included within *The Psalter 1998*?

Yes ☐ No ☐

(b) Which style(s) of music do you use for singing the psalms in worship?
Tick as many as apply.

Anglican chant ☐
Gregorian chant ☐
Metrical psalms ☐
Responsorial psalms ☐
Other (please state) ☐

Not sung ☐

Pointing

4 (a) In what ways, if any, could the styles of pointing used in the Music Appendix be improved?

(b) Which style of pointing do you prefer?

Anglican chant ☐
Plainchant ☐
Br. Reginald SSF ☐
Underlining ☐

Other (please state)

General

5   Do you have any other comments about *The Psalter 1998*?
      Please write on a separate sheet of A4 paper if necessary.

Name... Date.................................

Address...

....

Parish or equivalent...

Diocese...